SUSSEX
SEAMS
TWO

a further collection of

travel writing

CONSULTANT EDITOR

Dr Brian Short

Dean of School of Cultural and Community Studies
University of Sussex

SUSSEX SEAMS TWO

a further collection of travel writing

EDITED BY PAUL FOSTER

Foreword

by

IAN ELLIOTT

University College Chichester

West Sussex County Council

2000

Though we travel the world over to find the beautiful
we must carry it with us or we find it not

Ralph Waldo Emerson

A book is a book, but a good travel book is more than that -
it is a fine read, and an education

Rudyard Kipling

Forget, if you can, all your maps, guide-books,
historical and archaeological treatises.
Remember instead some little Downland path
which you could not stop to explore

Barclay Wills

FOREWORD

Travelling on the steam train up the Adur valley to school at Steyning, walking the South Downs and visiting communities across the county on behalf of the County Council, I am continually struck by the attraction of our countryside and of our towns and villages.

The essays and images contained in this volume help us better to understand what it is that makes our corner of England so special. It results from a pioneering collaboration between University College Chichester and the County Council and is a good example of how academic institutions and government can work together to produce something of real value to local communities. Sense of place is vital to all of us and *Sussex Seams Two* will help both residents and visitors to better understand the county which we all love.

Having lived in West Sussex for most of my life, I am very much aware of just how special a county it is.

Ian Elliott
September 1999

Chairman
West Sussex County Council

CONTENTS

INTRODUCTION

This volume of travel writing, as with its predecessor, *Sussex Seams* (1996), derives from two convictions - firstly, that there is as much interest to be found in our own county and region as in any distant or exotic location; and secondly, that to discover the reality of a people and a landscape, one needs more than one guide.

Both of these beliefs are at variance with current practice. Walk into any good book shop, ask for 'Travel' and it is probable that one will be directed to two sections - either to Travel Guides and Maps, or to Travel Literature. The former is not to the present purpose - we all know how to reach Guadeloupe or darkest Peru (just go to the travel agent and make a reservation) and, world travellers as so many of us are today, we can walk the boulevards of Paris and the piazzas in Pisa, the streets of Taipei and Sydney, without a guide; it is the latter that invites scrutiny. Scan the shelves, finger the covers, read the flaps - and marvel at the invitations: *Beyond the Sky and the Earth* (but few of us can be ready for the 'above' or the 'below'); *Signs of the Heart* (but such walk with me daily and I have no need to travel to hear them); or, least appealing of all, *Borders Up: Eastern Europe through the bottom of a glass* (for no glass that I have ever used fails, one way or another, to distort, to mock, or to aggrandize - and I prefer simpler pleasures).

Exhausted, we turn away and pause for thought: stimulating and challenging as the work of the more recognized authors is - one thinks of Norman Douglas, Jan Morris, Bruce Chatwin, Jonathan Raban, Dervla Murphy (and their successors, writers such as Nicolas Cave, Amitav Ghosh, Caryl Phillips), one wonders whether a volume of travel writing from various authors, devoted to what one might call 'a mosaic of home territory', would be possible.

One of the limitations of living in a particular region for any length of time is familiarity, the dulling of observation, such that we cease not only *to see,* but even to learn. Moving about our daily tasks, whether in village or town, within or without a region (and for the present purpose my declared region is Sussex, the historic county),* routine becomes dominant and one's surroundings become ever more 'porous' - blocks of buildings, entanglements of commercial, of social and political structures, through and round which we travel in order to achieve our own particular purposes. But these purposes constrain reflection, and if we seek to understand what is enduring in our lives and our history, we need to lengthen our perspective across both time and space, and become open to what has been termed 'alterity' - an engagement with what stands outside ourselves. To do that requires work[†] - listening to voices not our own, welcoming the anomalous, rejoicing in the accidental, and acknowledging that to engage in this way (even within our own domain of Sussex) may be uncomfortable. Indeed, as we read the contributions that follow, we will discover particularities, feelings, emotions that, although they are embedded in Sussex, are new, fresh, perhaps even incongruous.

But the pieces of a mosaic are never all the same shape and the same colour - or there would be no pattern - and in the

---

*Across the contributions to the present volume the bias is decidedly towards West Sussex locations. In saying that, I freely acknowledge it to be a restriction - but would argue that it is a necessary condition if one is to avoid any attempt at the comprehensive, which would only be specious. And one other thought: readers will notice, perhaps with surprise, that one topic, cricket, is treated three times, and that another is treated twice - which is a reminder that no single view is complete. An alternative way to make this last point is to be reminded that both history and literature (and I think culture more broadly) is to do with continuity and with echo: it is only the uninformed who deal in the pristine.

[†]At first thought such a view may be thought strange; but the word 'travel' has a common origin with the source of the word 'travail', and it was only when travelling became easy that the two meanings became separated and recognized through a difference in spelling.

mosaic that is *Sussex Seams Two* the pattern that emerges suggests three axes for consideration: style, chronology, and cultural diversity. Take style first: invited to write a piece of travel writing, some contributors saw an opportunity to write a critical essay on a figure who either visited Sussex, or lived here and expressed that experience in word or image (see, for example, John Wyatt about Coleridge, Timothy J. McCann about S.P.B. Mais, and Julian Marshall about G. Herbert Catt); while others chose to write a piece of imaginative fiction (see Patrick Garland's contribution, 'On the Road to Arras'). Similar differences occur if we think of the second axis, chronology: Syd Kelly chooses to write about a distant historical figure (Richard Cobden) and Molly Mahood about the less distant, at least in years, Kipling, whereas other contributors share a contemporary experience of today - Andrew Flaherty riding the South Downs Way, for example, and Chris Waters walking the Cuckmere Valley.* And if, lastly, we think of the third axis, cultural diversity defined in terms of what is indigenous or non-indigenous, even greater differences emerge: whereas John Godfrey, despite an opening reference to something French, writes solely of pattern in the Sussex countryside, and Rilla Dudley, in meditative poetry, interpenetrates the human with the living presences of chalk downland, Christopher Smith, in contrast, reveals in Sussex the lives of people from Vietnam, and Gaynor Williams shares with us, in a woodland setting associated with one of the historic Sussex estates (Goodwood), an experience - also from the East - of India. Nevertheless, taken together, this variety of prose, poetry, and image (much of which also reveals the contrasts present in the county) offers a map of Sussex that is unique, but also true.

---

*In pointing up this difference of chronology, we need also to note the skill with which both Kelly and Mahood reveal the interest and relevance of their chosen figure to present-day issues. Vivid examples of this link between the past and an experience of today is given in the work of two of the poets in the collection - Stephanie Norgate and Anne Williamson.

And although this assemblage of landscape, of incident, of belief, all of which was born in Sussex, may already - having been written - passed us by and now exist only in history, there is, in that very passing, a coherence - a declaration of where we were, what we have shared, and hence an affirmation of who we are now.

Paul Foster
27 August 1999

University College Chichester
Bishop Otter Campus

ONE

SHOREHAM AIRPORT

Tim Chilcott

There can be few places in Sussex, perhaps indeed anywhere, that are not invested with some sense of time. On occasions, the feeling may be grounded in basic, natural rhythms: seasonal changes from spring to summer, autumn to winter, or the cycle from day to night. On other occasions, it may derive from more obviously human perceptions of memory, actuality, and expectation - those constructions of past, present and future that our minds fashion to come to terms with the irresistibility of time's flow. Then again, some places seem to the imagination haunted by time - the age-old churches of Sussex, the ancient barrows and forts of the South Downs - while others appear immune - the faceless estate that neither develops nor decays, that is the same in rain or sunshine, summer or winter. Some places seem to be most alive, most quickeningly themselves, at special periods of the year or the day that inevitably pass - the late afternoon shaft of winter light on a stone wall, the blue-grey mist rising at dawn over the Arun. On others, time sits permanently, without deflection or arbitration. If you know the place at all, you know it only through the single eye of time. In these and many similar ways, the landscapes of Sussex are also timescapes, registering the wash of past, present and future over the terrain that is the South Country.

Often enough, the relationship between place and time can seem easy and automatic - a formulaic pairing of any spot with its natural equivalent in time. So, time past saturates church and castle, chalk-pit and combe. The present is caught, blankly, in the grey, non-identity of the latest shopping mall, that blurs into every other shopping mall that has ever been built. The future is snatched in the new cyber-café, or the rare soaring wings of a genuinely 21st century building, or the thrust and accelerations of a major airport like Gatwick. Such equations are unexceptional. But there are others, less self-evident, that disturb expectations. Here, time and place do not so much collude as collide. And nowhere in Sussex is such a collision more evocatively realized that in a place that seems to belie both its name and its time. Its full, official title is 'Brighton & Hove and Worthing joint municipal airport (Shoreham)'; and the convolution of name is an apt reflection of the disturbance of time that it evokes. For its atmosphere is not that of an airport, but of an aerodrome, even an airfield. And the difference between the three terms is of course crucial. If the prevailing spirit of airports is time future, the genius of aerodromes and airfields lies elsewhere, in some other province of time.

The airfield at Shoreham is almost always approached from the north, a turning off the A27 trunk road that connects many of the major coastal towns of Sussex. The approach is conventional, replicated in grander scale a thousand times in those motorways, autobahns, expressways, that point off to the often sprawling airport complexes close by. But a far more telling access to Shoreham is from the south. An unobtrusive sign leads you along a frequently pot-holed, almost single-track road, past a derelict World War II gun emplacement post, on to what was once a salt marsh, and then under the bridge that carries the railway west from Brighton towards Worthing, Chichester and beyond. The dip down under the bridge is often flooded, and the entire road is officially closed at night. But just up beyond the bridge, you come upon the airfield, its mere six-foot height above sea level barely holding back, so it seems, the waters of the Adur to the east, or the English Channel to the south. It was to these levels that, many years ago, a certain Harold Hume Piffard returned, remembering the place from his schooldays at Lancing

College, which overlooks the spot. He had already gained some fame as a music-hall entertainer and then as a portrait painter exhibiting at the Royal Academy. His skills in technical and mechanical design were said by a friend to be negligible; but to the flats at Shoreham he brought a pusher biplane, designed by himself and based upon a smaller model, driven by elastic, that had crashed within yards of taking off. In his full-scale biplane, though, Harold Piffard flew the first flight at Shoreham. It was May 1910, less than seven years after the Wright brothers had flown the first heavier-than-air plane in America.

Piffard was invariably, and unsurprisingly, addressed as 'Piff'; and if he now seems a worthy symbol of the first years of flying at Shoreham, it is because his nervy, exuberant personality (he was said to jump naked off bridges as trains approached, and always to smoke heavily before taking off) perfectly captures the atmosphere of carnival and escapade that pervaded the place. Upon the official opening of the airfield the following year, 1911, plans were presented to build a swimming pool, a tea garden and a bandstand on the site, with an area set aside for tennis courts and a croquet lawn. So popular an entertainment did the airfield become that it was necessary to build an eight-foot corrugated metal fence along the eastern and northern boundaries to deter unwanted sightseers. Even the actual business of flying had its own festivity. The airfield was one of the staging posts in the great Circuit of Europe and Circuit of Britain air races of 1911. And in July of that year, the first air cargo flight in Britain took off from Shoreham to deliver a case of Osram light bulbs to Marine Park in Hove, where it landed before a rapturous crowd of 5,000. The flight was accomplished in a monoplane with the somehow curiously appropriate name of Valkyrie.

But if the three or four years before World War I marked Shoreham's infancy, it was the three or four years before World War II that marked its golden youth. In 1936, the airfield was rejuvenated as a centre of private and civil aviation with a classic art deco terminal that survives intact as a Grade II listed building. To arrive and go inside is at once to relive the enchantment - sometimes innocent, sometimes sophisticated, always carefree - of flying in the thirties. No cavernous, impersonal departure hall, no plastic phalanx of check-in desks, no queues at security control, but a simple and proportionate atrium, with a single counter facing you for the receipt of tickets and luggage. Above, at first-floor level, a balcony runs along the four sides of the concourse, and an unpretentious chandelier hangs from a domed, sky-blue ceiling. To the left of the atrium, the restaurant; to the right, what was once the customs hall; and ahead, through just one set of doors, the airfield itself. The whole feel of the place is of easy domestic comfort, an effortless transition of scarcely thirty yards from the motor-car that has delivered you at the front of the building to the aeroplane at the back, ready to carry you skyward.

Shoreham Airport archive

THE APRON OF SHOREHAM AIRPORT: SUMMER 1936
Visitors enjoy refreshments as a D.H. 89A Rapide of
Railway Air Services is about to leave

Skyward from Shoreham in the 1930s was a popular and fashionable activity. Cecil Pashley who, with his brother Eric, had founded a flying school and aeroclub at Shoreham in 1913, consolidated its success in his South Coast Flying Club. The airfield continued as a staging-post in numerous air races; and several airlines also operated services on domestic routes. In 1936, it was possible to fly from Shoreham to Bournemouth, Bristol, Cardiff, Croydon, Liverpool, Manchester, Portsmouth and Ryde, as well as (more exotically) to Jersey, Deauville and Le Touquet. There were even more wide-flung adventures. After the outbreak of war in September 1939, international airline operators were removed from the old London aerodrome at Croydon down to Sussex, from where, remarkably, flights continued to Paris and Amsterdam until the beginning of the Blitzkrieg. But perhaps most romantic of all was the service opened by Imperial Airways on 22 September 1939 from Shoreham, via Marseilles, Tunis, Malta and Sollum, to Alexandria. To read its schedule of arrival and departure times is, even now, to feel that catch at the heart as a real journey is begun. You flew only in the morning or early afternoon, and then rested overnight. It was three and a half hours to Marseilles, a further three and a quarter to Tunis. You landed and took off on five separate occasions before you reached your destination. On a flight that would today take less than five hours, you were in the air for fourteen hours and three minutes. And then, in June 1940, when a war suddenly became less than phoney, the journey could no longer be made.

If Shoreham's position during wartime seems now to have been relatively undramatic, it is perhaps because its peacetime domesticity was translated so fluently into a wartime role. Its primary function in the First World War was as a training school for fledgling pilots, in the Second as a centre for air-sea rescue. In both, its history was quiet and honourable, notably in support of the D-day invasion of 1944. But war did not change it. It brushed against momentousness, contributed unstintingly what it could, but kept somehow an

OUTBOUND						INBOUND
Thursday	1030	*dep*	SHOREHAM	*arr*	1152	
	1352	*arr*	MARSEILLES	*dep*	0830	Thursday
Friday	0900	*dep*	MARSEILLES	*arr*	1341	
	1215	*arr*	TUNIS	*dep*	1026	
	1315	*dep*	TUNIS	*arr*	0926	
	1441	*arr*	MALTA	*dep*	0800	Wednesday
Saturday	0700	*dep*	MALTA	*arr*	1300	
	1114	*arr*	SOLLUM	*dep*	0846	
	1214	*dep*	SOLLUM	*arr*	0746	
	1400	*arr*	ALEXANDRIA	*dep*	0600	Tuesday

ALL TIMES ARE GMT

SHOREHAM - ALEXANDRIA: *September 1939- June 1940*

older spirit - of ordinary flyers on a common soil, working the days through that made up their lives, without striking glamour or epic exploit. Indeed, there could be no better symbol of the airfield's war-time role than the D-day museum that now stands at its south-eastern edge. The exhibits inside - gas-masks, ration-books, propellers, letters, cockpits, photographs - movingly evoke the passionate commonness of it all, the simple heroisms that became an individual and instinctual way of feeling. And outside, hard against the corrugated roof of the Nissen hut that houses the museum, there is a row of roses, each bush marked with an individual's name, that riotously blooms in June.

But finally, of course, when all the many contours of history have been traced, you cannot but follow the example of your countless predecessors, and fly into the air yourself. The main runway of today, some 3,000 feet long, could accommodate business jets or medium-sized turbo prop aircraft. But, far better, go up in a small plane, a Cessna 152 or 172, a Piper Warrior or Tomahawk. The first time you climb into the cockpit, the immediate sense is how near everything is. No longer now some distant apparatus for flying locked away behind unopened doors, but a row of instruments, dials, knobs, levers, all within arm's reach: altimeter, air speed, heading, artificial horizon, radio frequency. And once clearance for take-off is given and the plane rolls down runway 21, the next sense is how slow yet how effortless this primal clutch at the air is. At less than 60 knots, a slight easing back on the control column, and the plane is air-borne. It all seems to have taken scarcely a breath of wind. Up to fifty, a hundred, two hundred feet, and now the sky is all that can be seen through the front cockpit windows. A bank to starboard, and the runway suddenly comes into view, a thin line of dark grey, narrowing with every moment. And then the ground slips more and more away, and the designs of the landscape compose themselves and become intelligible. As you gain height, you notice its shapes and connections: the tiny square of sunburst-yellow rape offset by the parallelogram of grassland, the half circle of dullish white chalk in the fold of the hill, the ribbon of human habitation poking out like a thumb into downland. And then, as the plane settles itself in level flight, comes the time when earth and air seem to surrender their separate identities, and to take on some new and other role.

It is never easy to know at what height this will occur, or when. Certainly, it is never at 35,000 feet, when the earth from a 747 or Airbus 300 is simply a distant redundancy. Even at 10,000 feet, the earth remains flattened, regularised within a two-dimensional axis of length and breadth, yet without depth. But somewhere perhaps between 2,000 and 3,000 feet, the pits and hollows, slopes and banks of the land are as clearly visible as the lowest wisps of straggling cloud, or the infinite gradations of the sky's colours from blinding white to blood-purple and red. You murmur the names of the settlements below like some talisman - Findon, Arundel, Amberley, Storrington - and find their silent mirrors in the cloud shapes above. At this height, sky and earth have become proportionate, attuned to each other, coalesced. The moment of joining may occur at earliest light, or noon, or twilight; but it is always magical.

You want to stay in that time and that space, hung between heaven and earth, the plane's wings now effortlessly yours. From this height, the world seems perfect and whole, all its crazy multiplicities drawn together into a single sight, all its fretting quietened. But ultimately, however beguiling the vision, you know the order you've witnessed is specious. The haphazard plenitude of the earth calls you back. And as you slowly descend past fifteen, fourteen, thirteen hundred feet, you begin to distinguish again the distinctiveness of things. Individual streets become identifiable, crops told apart, streams noticed; and matchstick figures regain a human stature. The plane banks from its down-wind leg to soar over Beeding Hill and then Mill Hill, the high points on the Downs crossed on the major approach path. And then the control-column is eased forward, engine power reduced, flaps extended, and the plane dips down to land. As the wheels hover over and then touch the runway, you know you're back where you belong, in your natural element of earth. But no landing is ever without some murmur of loss, some ancient pull urging you to go back up there, in the high, blue-white air. It is like a half-remembered call of soaring eagles.

Every year, hundreds of planes take off and land at Shoreham, repeating a pattern that has existed for nearly ninety years. To all intents and purposes, the place has witnessed our century. To a part of the mind, it lives most, perhaps, in special times: its very beginnings, the mid-1930s, the second world war years. But elsewhere in the imagination, it is its very ordinariness that confers the romance. It is a place without rhetoric - whether of size, or achievement, or ambition. Its atmosphere is easy and accessible and unostentatious. To find its centre, you do not need to fly, nor even, strangely, to visit the airfield itself. But go to the top of Mill Hill on a hot, windless afternoon of high summer. Below you are the last glittering bends of the Adur before it reaches the sea, and across its valley, the spires of Lancing College Chapel and the rounding slopes of Lancing mystical culture and hence important to the success of the tourist industry. The sense of magic and mystery in the alchemy and astrological branches of knowledge is a potent subtext that underpins India. India is apparently one thing, but actually another. Or, maybe it is the two? In reality, of course, it is many-faceted. Yet, before passing to the second work that evokes the spirit of India, there is more to be considered, for the vital missing parts from *The Two of Us* are the heads. This omission is, of itself, strange, disturbing, and even more so in the case of the elephant-forms since it is the elephant head that precisely embodies and makes the Indian god, Lord Ganesh, identifiable. Lord Ganesh (the god of new beginnings) may not be familiar to white Anglo-Saxons of a certain age but there is a burgeoning interest in the spiritual as opposed to the religious at the close of our turbulent century.

Stephen Cox's sculpture, *Granite Catamarans on a Granite Wave* (1994), is just that, since the work has been created by the earliest method of making sculpture - carving; it comprises many parts and has been described as being

GRANITE CATAMARANS ON A GRANITE WAVE (1994)
Stephen Cox

steeped in myth and history, and transports the viewer through an entirely different set of factors to those present in Gregory's work. Moreover, it has had its own convoluted journey, one of which is its change of name. Commissioned by Wilfrid and Jeannette Cass, it was originally called *Yatra* and was inspired by catamarans riding a majestic wave. Then there is the fact that the granite was transported from India, an occurrence which resulted from Cox representing Britain in the Indian Triennale in 1985 at the invitation of the British Council. It was this that led Cox to set up a workshop in India (one of the ancient stone-carving civilisations) and subsequently discover an innate passion for the sub-continent. But of all these factors perhaps the most apposite in terms of the current theme is the extraordinary fragility the sculptor manages to instill in the granite boats atop the granite waves. The sense of interdependence is apparent - without the waves the boat would not travel, the sea could still exist (and provide sustenance for the unseen creatures within) but notwithstanding there is a sense that without the boat the sea would be functionless - at least in this work, as it would be reduced to a series of pillars spaced in a meaningful fashion but the meaning would remain hidden. However, there is water and the paradox of water being the giver and taker of life is particularly associated with the Hindu system of belief, offering evidence of Cox's knowledge and passion for both classical and Indian myth. There are a number of journeys here and the setting for this piece at the boundary of the park allows the viewer to embark.

Dhruva Mistry's work, *The Object* (1995-97) is assembled or constructed, a method of making invented by Picasso; and it is Picasso's work which initiated the massive shift in the world of 3D forms from the process of 'taking away' (carving, or carving as a preliminary to casting) to the process of 'building up': the idea of 'the object' had arrived and this, very neatly, is the title of Mistry's work. Constructed from stainless steel, it is the manifestation of a paradox. In some ways it

of glass makers huts in hogwood and sometimes we walk along the wey and arun canal and i think this is perfect just perfect and sometimes we see another area of woodland being cleared for a house

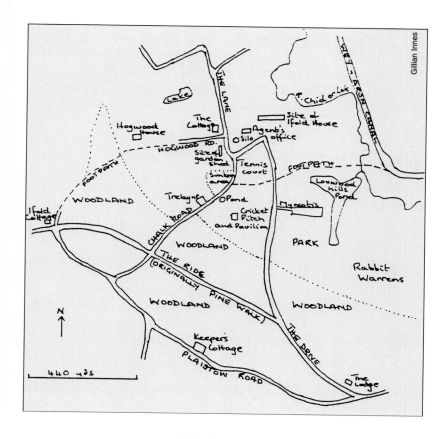

IFOLD IN THE 1930s

In 1934 the estate was marked off in plots of not less than one-third acre. Plots on the cricket pitch were £40 per acre and those on the parkland £50 per acre. Building was spasmodic, but by 1990, all the plots had been sold. In the past few years developers have bought 'back lands' and built closes of five-bedroomed houses selling at approximately £350,000.

my son says the quince tree will have to come down no i say it cant but mum he says the roots are all over the patio and thats why its cracked come and look and you wouldn't believe how far those roots have stretched and arched and prodded theyre like living fingers

but the tree must be very old i say it seems wrong to chop it down but the men say theres no point putting down new flagstones for that old crone of a tree to push them up again so i agree and they chop her down but when we find the token and work out how old the tree is i feel as if ive mugged

Diana Mitchener

THE BREWERS
TOKEN
(1794)

an old lady connie connie i say weve found an old coin oh she says how old mmcmxciv i say oh she says say it again and then she says that is 1794 and oh id love to see it so i take it to connies house that she built herself with her own hands and its called myosotis and it was one of the first plots sold in ifold in 1934 for fifty pounds per acre but now they are chopping down woodland and building houses for over three hundred thousand pounds oh says connie i think it is sad how the place has changed and our gardens are full of magpies and connie has written a book on local history and she knows about tokens

oh says connie this is a brewers token but it ceased to be legal
tender after they brought in monetary union in england
scotland and wales in 1797 oh i said it is just like the euro and
who wants it anyway in 1794 says connie mints couldnt
supply enough coins and the merchants hadnt enough small
change so the traders made tokens with their own symbols
like a loaf for a baker but no kings head but its as if the old
token had waited in the ground to spring up two hundred
years later at the end of the century

when people are talking about monetary union again

oh says connie you must take it to sothebys to get it valued so
i do

what the man from sothebys said

you are correct in your surmise that this is a token of a type in
circulation before the redesign and redistribution of new
coinage during the reign of william the third
as such i regret it is of low value and would be of little interest
to a collector
i would place its value at four pounds, although you might
raise marginally more at its place of origin

thank god for that i said to sam as we got back in the car that
means we can keep it
alison says she places a coin in the roots of a new tree so now
i am convinced that this is why the token was there and that
it was not just lost which i thought first

what are you doing lionel asks its three oclock in the morning
cant you sleep how can i tell him that im moving flagstones
around in my head and that and some are flawed - but if i take
them out i lose the past-future link in the poem

and if i change daniels name to roy thatd be a good idea then id have a run roy roi king reign rain puddles well underneath the lines to symbolise the roots and theres time thyme not mint yes mint or rue yes or there is sorrel sorrel is nice sorrel sorry yes regret miss sorrel is ok

so what else do i like about the tree i like the bark and how it changes colour in the sunshine it is gold not gold more bronze no that is dull more copper yes copper and arthritic but that wont fit but the trunk is knobbled and bent and twisted crippled i could use crippled and that is true of lionel also now

THE TOKEN

I

Piggy-banked beneath the quince
gathering interest for two hundred years:
a brewer's token, 1794.

Pressed in the sapling's roots by the old well
to wish the tree long life and swelling fruit
or lost in a wager, spinning to the soil

to be un-earthed by lager-drinking lads
prizing the roots up, chopping down the tree,
labour rewarded with this half-pence coin.

II

We filled the well with stones when Roy was small
and paved the yard so he could safely hop
through puddles when the rain stopped. I regret

the loss of the rose garden's ragged grass
to slabs of pavement, jig-sawed through the years
with trailing sorrel, knots of mint and thyme.

Each spring I miss the quince, the pink
curled blossom, crippled copper bark,
the sharp out-dated flavour of its fruit.

III
What's the coin worth? It's value-less, I say,
a labourer's wage two hundred years ago.
My daughter's hands close over it. She's still
lost in the presence of another life:
his hands to hers, a gift in crumbling clay
unchanged with age, a present from the past.

THE BREWER'S TOKEN
1794
with one new penny, Roman coins and
a Roman lamp

> We place the token by the Roman lamp
> and Nana's thimble, while outdoors the men
> lay Pennistone flags, £2.95 plus VAT

youd think lionel would slow down now hes retired but he cant stop making things and he makes chess sets for all our family one set each and he casts friezes and cherubs and we stick them up all over the walls and ceilings in the old part of the house youd laugh if you saw how many youll have to change the name of the house to the encrusted cottage i say and charge admission and what am i going to do with all these quinces asks my sister make jelly or something i say there are more than i can use but in the last few years there are hardly any and lionel makes fewer and fewer figures because he hasnt the energy and in the last year there is only one quince on the tree and lionel says its had it

why am i fretting i ask myself it was just a crippled old tree but i keep thinking about the quince and the petals and the way the bark had a copper sheen on it in the sun so you forgot how twisted and old it was and now theres an ache where it used to be

i didnt realise when i began the poem that the token and the tree were so symbolic for me i am getting almost obsessed by them and the close of the century too i cant bear to think about it dont talk yourself into a panic mum now dont daniel says and he is right but he will leave next year and sam will leave in the spring they must lead their own lives it is time but the new century will be different for me and for the country too and the coinage will change and i think the european union is a terrible mistake and how things will be two hundred years from now no one can tell

Note:
For a history of Ifold, see Bayley, C., *Ifold, Loxwood and Plaistow: Forgotten Border Villages* (Ifold and District Local History Society) 1988.

F O U R

Bishop's Garden, Chichester

Denise Bennett

Usually they are called
cotton reel, log cabin or church window
but this coverlet
worked from a photograph
I have named Bishop's Garden;
the place where by daughter
used to play - years ago

A spot for shoppers, lovers
and families to gather
under the shadow of a spire,
to admire the scented shrubs,
and the bright borders.
I remember the time when she came
tacking through the wet grass
and how we imagined
'the Selfish Giant tree ...'

For two summers I have stitched
the honeycomb flowers
matching the fabric to catch the sun.
Making a marriage vestment
of violet and rose.
Each hexagonal petal
sensual enough for any bee.

F I V E

Roger Bamber: OUSE VALLEY VIADUCT, NEAR BALCOMBE (1999)

The viaduct was built in 1839 by the London, Brighton South Coast Railway, and cost £50,000; Railtrack has now just spent four years in restoration at a cost of £6 million. There are 37 arches in all, across a length of 1475 ft, and they stand 100 ft high; the whole structure comprises 11.3 million bricks. The photograph shows brickwork quantifiers checking the repointing and replacement.

SIX

Sussex Village Cricket

Brian Caws

Travel across the county during summer weekends and you will almost certainly pass a number of village cricket matches, for village cricket is part of summer and part of Sussex. It is on Sundays, in 1999, that you see the real village cricket in the county as Saturdays tend to be devoted to 'league matches' rather unlovely events with complicated rules and 'points', anathema to any genuine village cricketer. The game today is neither as rustic nor as pure and high-minded as some writers would have you believe but it still takes you into the heart of Sussex, it still unites young and old - no generation gap here - and it still contains a rich blend of humour, endeavour, skill and basic, decent humanity.

There is a wandering side in this part of Sussex called 'The Falling Leaves'. The idea, originally, was that it should be restricted to the over-40s, hence the name; Kent has a similar team called, rather more imaginatively perhaps, 'The Guttering Candles'. The over-40 rule is no longer strictly observed as over-40s have sons who can actually run and bend and so prove invaluable, but the fixture list gives a good idea of the Sussex scene, albeit that some have the misfortune to be just over the Hampshire or Surrey border: Eartham and Boxgrove, Ebernoe, Compton, Rogate, Steep, Tillington, Stedham, Singleton, Watersfield, Chiddingfold, Buriton, Kirdford, Lynchmere, Lurgashall, Elsted and Trotton, Fittleworth, Harting and Slindon . . . *sic transit gloria mundi* - more of Slindon in a moment.

To drive back on a summer's evening after an afternoon spent on any of these grounds is to experience Sussex at its mellow and amiable best. They all have their particular merits but let us narrow the focus and look more closely at just one of them, Ebernoe.

If you travel along the A283, leaving Petworth, and head north towards the A3 and Guildford, you will, after about three miles, see a sign on the right to Ebernoe. Take this turning, and you will find yourself on a narrow, winding road with some pleasant houses set back in wooded seclusion and then, suddenly, on an open green where the road runs through (through, not by or round) a cricket ground. If it is

Brian Caws

EBERNOE CRICKET GROUND
The road bisects the ground, even during play

summer and if a match is in progress, you will, if a thoughtful driver, wait until a break in the play. If you are not a thoughtful driver, you can find a white-clad figure moving rapidly across your bows in pursuit of the ball. You will not find Ebernoe itself even if you survive your transit of the cricket field for this was one of the Sussex villages wiped out by the plague. What remains are some scattered, highly desirable residences and a tiny chapel. It has been described by Pevsner as 'an improbable, enchanted place in the middle of the Weald' - but it does have a cricket team and, in many ways, it is a model of a Sussex village side. The ground, despite the intruding road, is idyllic, surrounded by woods, with a pleasant, rustic pavilion and a cottage complete with orchards. The cottage owners have, only recently, adopted the defensive measure of placing wire mesh screens over vulnerable windows - a sensible precaution as the Ebernoe team contains some sturdy hitters. The wicket is pitched E - W, necessarily parallel with the road, which means that a visiting side batting after tea on a clear summer's evening will find the ball being tossed high into the path of the setting sun by the crafty Ebernoe slow bowlers, leading to temporary blindness for a batsman at the eastern end and a rapid conclusion to the game. If the visitors find themselves in the field after tea, then the nature of the Ebernoe tea itself provides the home team with the advantage. Afternoon tea is fast disappearing from the English social scene but not at village cricket matches and certainly not at Ebernoe. The lavish nature of the fare means that visitors almost always over-indulge and this leads to a somnolent mood during the evening session, an attitude not conducive to athletic prowess. Either way, both teams are usually down at the excellent local hostelry in neighbouring Balls Cross in good time. Ale no longer flows as freely as it once did (modern drink-driving laws) but the local pub is still the place to re-live the day's events and to renew annual contact with friendly opponents.

Despite the generally relaxed nature of the game, rivalry between villages can be strong. Ebernoe's particular 'local derby' is with Lurgashall, a few miles away. Lurgashall is an English picture-book village. If you have American visitors, take them to Lurgashall. The village green is surrounded by well-kept, expensive houses, a converted village school, the village stores, the church and the village pub. It is a rich village, close enough for Haslemere or Guildford commuters and the rivalry with the local lads of Ebernoe is natural and inevitable. Lurgashall has a vineyard and an annual open-air drama production in July, usually Shakespeare, but then, Ebernoe has its annual Horn Fair on the cricket ground, in August. Rivalry on the cricket field is no doubt a more civilised development from more remote days when regular raids were made between Sussex villages - Stopham, Kirdford and Wisborough Green being particularly prominent in this activity - in order to rape the girls. David Atkins, in his book *The Cuckoo in June*, tells of these raids and writes: 'I am sure it is based on fact and, over a thousand years, was nature's way of avoiding inter-breeding in an area where travel was very difficult because of the heavy clay'. It would be nice to think that a Darwinian concern for the survival of the species, coupled with the structure of the soil, was the main motive.

Ebernoe was one of the villages raided in this way, but Ebernoe was not one of the more popular resorts as it specialised in the production of dwarfs. Ebernoe dwarfs became quite famous throughout England and on the Continent and there were always a number for sale at the Horn Fair in the fifteenth and sixteenth centuries. The juice of knotgrass, the dwarf elder, and the daisy, can all be used to stunt growth and Ebernoe seems to have cornered a lucrative market for a time. Perhaps Shakespeare had the village in mind when he wrote, in *A Midsummer Night's Dream* -

> Get you gone, you dwarf,
> You minimus, of hindering knotgrass made.

The present-day village cricket team, one should perhaps add, shows not the slightest evidence of the past expertise of the area. Similar stories could be told about many Sussex villages and, indeed, are told, many of them after cricket matches on a summer's evening, for village cricket somehow encourages reminiscence and nostalgia. There is a sense of being part of a way of life that goes back over centuries. Sussex is not alone in this, of course. Francis Thompson, better known for *Hound of Heaven*, thinking of Yorkshire when he was living in the South of England, wrote:

> And I look through my tears at a soundless-clapping host
> As the run-stealers flicker to and fro,
> To and fro.

The beautifully-chosen word 'flicker' in this context - the word of a poet - takes the reader immediately back into the past cricket has a history that reflects the history of the nation itself. There is no need to look further afield than Chichester:

> I present Ralphe West, Edward Hartley, Richard Slaughter, William Martin, Richard Martin jun. together with others in their company whose names I have no notice of, for playing at cricket in the churchyard on Sunday the fifth of May, after sufficient warnings given to the contrary to the 7th Article, secondly that they used to break the church windows with the ball and, thirdly, for that a little childe had like to have her braynes beaten out with a cricket bat.
>
> And also I present Richard Martin sen. and Thomas West, the old churchwardens for defending and mayntayning them in it and Edward Hartley, for playing at cricket in evening prayer tyme on Sunday the XXVII of April.
> (*Bills of Presentment of parishioners to the Right Reverend Bishop of Chichester, 1622*)

The Martins, the Wests and the Hartleys look to have posed difficult problems for the righteous and we can only assume that the term 'old' when applied to churchwardens here means 'ex'. The mind boggles at the image of 'Richard

Slaughter' - a wonderful name for an Australian fast bowler. Apart from the somewhat sinister reference to the 'little childe', however, this seems very much in the tradition of the village cricket match. Even today, there are villages where the game has to end before 6.30. pm. (that is, before Evensong) and cricket balls and glass still keep uneasy company. But look at the date. One would imagine that there was a lean period for such disgraceful behaviour between 1640 and 1660 but there is evidence of organized cricket near *The Plough Inn* at Upper Dicker in 1677 and of matches between Goodwood and Arundel in 1702. Most people, among the minority of the population who have any views at all on the subject, associate the birth of cricket - and therefore the birth of village cricket - with Hampshire and Hambledon. The beginnings of the game remain uncertain and need not concern us here. Enough that Neville Cardus, a fine writer on music and cricket, neatly side-steps the issue by stating that the game 'began in Kent, Sussex, Hampshire and London'. As far as this part of Sussex is concerned, Goodwood and Slindon figure strongly in early records and in 1744, Slindon played a team that was probably London - the match was certainly played in London. A fortnight later, Slindon tackled Kent, the match being celebrated in the epic style by one James Love, who described cricket as:

O thou, sublime Inspirer of my Song

Shades of John Milton. It is hard to envisage such early matches when playing today against Slindon's modest and cheerful team, with fielders having to risk instant death in order to retrieve the ball whenever it is hit over or (worse) into a particularly lethal stretch of the A29. The mighty Hambledon itself declined, however, and now all that remains of its eighteenth-century glory (celebrated by another excellent prose writer, John Nyren) is a useful village side and an excellent pub, *The Bat and Ball*.

As the game increased in popularity, it became organized,

until today, when, like so many things, it is possibly over-organized. The laws were revised by the Mary-le-Bone Cricket Club (M.C.C.) in 1820, and, during the reign of Queen Victoria, cricket became legal. Before an Amending Act of 1845, the game was officially banned by Act of Parliament from the time of Henry VIII as a consequence of 'crafty persons having invented new and crafty games whereof archery is sore decayed'. Cricket still had its 'crafty persons, however, for betting was a significant part of matches, including Sussex village matches. Not now, of course. Very few village cricketers would have the confidence to put hard cash on any Sunday afternoon result.

The fact that the season begins with the promise of May and ends with the fading of Summer has always given the game a certain gentle sadness, reflected in the extract from Francis Thompson, but Thompson was not given to a particularly cheerful approach to human existence and, in general, the village teams of Sussex display a relaxed and balanced outlook on life. As A.G.MacDonnell observed, when describing a village cricket match in his excellent humorous novel, *England Their England*: 'Those whose lives are occupied in combating the eccentricities of God regard as very small beer the eccentricities of Man'. Village cricket remains an essential part of the Sussex summer scene. If it disappears, ousted by year-long football or baseball or motor cycle scrambling, the country and the county which can claim to have given it birth will have lost something that is an irreplaceable link with a living past.

SUNDAY 12TH
SEPTEMBER 1999

Ebernoe versus
'The Falling Leaves'

Brian Caws

No Carping Spirit:
G. Herbert Catt and Chichester
School of Art

Julian Marshall

'*Sketch books are very sensitive to, and are easily damaged by, Damp Atmosphere and Sea-Air.*' Who can be surprised if such a book (well used) has succumbed to 'Mildew and Spots' evidently cause of customer complaints to Winsor & Newton - after 104 years? It is now kept in the recommended position, well away from 'the influence of floors wet from washing', in Pallant House.

But Mr Catt's pocket would have been snug enough for this best of quality notebooks, neat in its hard covers and closed firmly by a band. Within are fine-pencil detailed drawings and a whole language of tiny cross-hatched headings, fillets, corbels and capitals carefully numbered to some esoteric scheme, clarifying to its inventor, but mystifying to the uninitiated. Here are recipes for brewing gesso, book-titles and skeleton lecture-notes. Tantalisingly not a single one is dated.

George Herbert Catt (1868-1920), founder of Chichester School of Art, was a Sussex man. He was born at Twineham, just west of the main London to Brighton road and north of the steep scarp of the Devil's Dyke. The farm house, 'Stuckles', must have been a very full family home; there were already three boys and two girls in the nursery when George was born in June 1868, and he was followed by two more brothers.

The house stands in open fields, back from the little meandering Twineham road and on a slight hill; canny positioning by its fourteenth-century builder, for on the day I visited, its reflection swam and stretched in the squally wind whipping over flooding, like a moat about the garden. Inside, an

STUCKLES FARM, Twineham
Julian Marshall

enormous hearth in the slab-paved sitting-room suggests that it was once a kitchen, or a modest Great Hall in its earliest days. A small wing has been added at the east side of the house - could this have been for the expanding Catt family? The exterior gives away little of the history of the building for now it is all 'Standen' country-house style: warm brick below and tile-hung above, with white-framed windows and a decidedly Arts and Crafts front door.

A very ordinary little pencilled drawing, among the designs for the wallpaper and dados nevertheless distinguishes itself, bearing that rare item, a label: 'boss, Farnham Church' it says, a useful pointer.

DIPPENHALL FARM,
Farnham
Julian Marshall

In 1879 the Catt family moved to Dippenhall Farm, near Farnham. While his two elder brothers helped work the farm and two elder sisters were young ladies, George aged eleven was dispatched (probably) to the Grammar School. Here George Sturt was teaching the first formers, drawing amongst his subjects. Encouraged, Catt took extra classes at the Art School, achieving his first Department Certificate aged sixteen. Like other provincial art schools of the South Kensington network, Farnham enjoyed 'loan of Books, Paintings and examples of Applied Art from the Victoria and Albert Museum'. At twenty Catt was teaching, assistant to Joseph Hill, and part of a flourishing and successful establishment with 'most favourable' examination results - which, the newspaper continues, reflect 'the greatest credit on Mr Hill and his assistant Mr George Catt'. Not so much to their credit was a studio double-booking causing a clash with the Gymnastic Club .... with 'disastrous effect'! I hope young Catt was not responsible.

Hill was succeeded by W.H.Allen, a man with a glowing reputation. He had distinguished himself at The Royal College of Art, winning the Gold Medal and expectations of an exceptional career ahead. Five years senior to Catt, he had already travelled abroad, working on commissions in Italy. In Farnham he found an existing group of intellectuals who, like Sturt, were much influenced by the ideas of Ruskin and Morris; very different preoccupations to those of the farming circle of Catt's home. On 17 November 1890, Sturt's Journal reports: 'George Catt came in, from 7 - 8 this evening a very true-natured man, much stuffed up with all sorts of old well-to-do religious prejudices: - which, however, he seems to be leaving more and more out in the cold. He was great [I thought this was modern speak] on a sermon he had heard last night ... as the sort of thing Ruskin might have written.'*

The two young artists were well placed to keep up with the trends of the capital's art scene: 'LIVE AT FARNHAM - Surrey Lanes, Pine Woods and Heather: FREQUENT FAST TRAINS' - which developers advertised, and the necessary visits to their H.Q. at South Kensington provided opportunity for more exciting explorations of 'Modern' galleries. Aubrey Beardsley may have shocked or delighted them, Art Nouveau had arrived from Europe, Tennyson's death (1892) was - it might be thought scandalously - marked by Wilde's *Lady Windermere's Fan* and Lottie Collins's music hall hit 'Ta-ra-ra-boom-de-ay' was whistled in the streets and sung at the

---

*All Sturt quotations are taken from E. D. Mackarness (ed.), *The Journals of George Sturt - 1890-1927* (1967).

silver leaves' flourished too, reminding him of his time on Norfolk Island, and a Banksia rose curtained his south wall: 'they were his comrades and knew his heart'. More exciting, for the young, was his experience of cannibalism . . . choirboys, I have been told, were enthralled by a glimpse of his heavily scarred ankle, evidence they did not doubt, of An Encounter of the Too-Close Kind. It is consoling to know that the old man's last wish was gratified. He expressed a longing to see his banana tree again: and, carried out into the garden, he looked at his friend from the South Seas and died.*

Autumn 1899 was a busy time for the Catt household in East Row. Amy was fully occupied with young Philip, born in October, and Catt with arrangements for moving his Art School from Crane Street into its new, purpose-built quarters above the Market House in North Street in the coming May. An upper floor had been added to John Nash's design of 1808,

* See *Dr H. R. Codrington* - pamphlet A1/1/5 (Cutten Collection) at West Sussex Record Office.

In 1900 Chichester School of Art moved into the newly erected Jubilee Memorial premises over John Nash's Butter Market (1808).
Note stairs to the Studios on left with sign over.

West Sussex Record Office

heavy cornices and classical pilasters repeating the original below. The niche on the left of the portico was opened up into a staircase leading to the two long, high-ceilinged studios, with the Principal's office on the right. A new four-page Prospectus was printed by J.W.Moore of East Street (Moore & Tillyer?) detailing the courses offered by 'The City of Chichester School of Art, Head Master G.Herbert Catt, Silver Medallist'. To reach this position at the age of thirty-two, Catt had spent eight years progressing through the rigid requirements of the all-powerful Department of Science and Art. Work produced for satisfying examiners in each of the 23 'stages' had to be sent to South Kensington; if successful it would be stamped with the magic roundel 'E.S.K. WORK ACCEPTED FOR CERTIFICATE'. Amongst the impressive stack of these certificates of Catt's are two belonging to his wife, Amy: one, dated 1884, matches his, indicating that they probably met at a Farnham art class that year.*

Today's free spirits entering art schools would be stunned by the prescriptive exercises laid down in the 'E.S.K.' curriculum. 'Drawing from the Cast, Shading from the Cast, Shading from Models, Linear Perspective, Plant Drawing in Outline, Painting Ornament in Monochrome' - the labour stretched unremittingly ahead. But to Catt and his fellows, the aim of this training, to establish a 'grammar' of work practice in crafts together with fine art, was an accepted concept. The flood of cheap 'decorative' goods of dubious quality and design which was mass-produced following the Great Exhibition of 1851 dismayed William Morris and others of what is now called The Arts and Crafts Movement. They tried to counteract this explosion of the shoddy by providing well-designed and functionally-excellent household furnishings of all kinds. And Catt joins in, '*We will have* our houses and churches and public buildings *decorated*. This love of

*Much of the Catt archive is now in the library at Pallant House, Chichester; there is also material at West Sussex Record Office (Acc. 9921).

decoration is innate and rightly so, but it needs guiding and cultivating the same as our other tastes, that it may have a refining and elevating influence on our lives . . . we should study Historic ornament reverently and in no Carping Spirit.'

In his notebook are jottings for a lecture at St. Michael's, Bognor, in 1901 - quite a harangue for school-leavers at fourteen! 'You will be leaving school and returning to your homes, and I want to influence you *there,* in years to come you will be having homes of your very own I want to influence you in the direction of *these new homes.'* He proceeds to discuss wallpaper and carpets: and of furniture, 'it shall be *well-built*: strength, dignity with the smallest amount of wood, treat wood expertly *as* wood' and he goes on to condemn Chippendale-style 'twiddles and turnings'.

By 1905 the Catt family was enlarged by the birth of Kenneth (1901) and Cicely (1904) and they had moved from No. 2 to the Depot House next door. In their day it adjoined the local Regimental H.Q., so perhaps young Kenneth was inspired by things military, for he later played the trumpet and joined the Army! Depot House - now Suffolk House Hotel - is certainly larger and its aspect lighter without Sadler's tall building opposite; but what of Catt's specially built studio left behind in the garden of No. 2? In conversion to an hotel the interior is much altered, but I believe their drawing-room was the handsome room with a grand fireplace and garden view, on the first floor. This would leave the two square rooms below for a combined study/studio: there is certainly evidence of arch- or door- ways connecting the two. The house stretches up to a cluster of small bedrooms, suitable for children and a maid, as well as down to brick-floored cellars where the weekly washerwoman toiled and where Catt kept his wines; from here a passage runs, connecting with tunnels from the Old Priory to the Grey Friars' burial ground in St John's Street.

None of this ancient history was in the mind of Mr Catt as he emerged from the neat pedimented doorway of his home. His upright figure, 'tall, bearded and bewiskered', recalls his

East Row from the Catts' door-step. Horse-drawn wagons were used until the 1920s. Sadler's Stables on the right by the boy on the pavement.

Wherefore art thou, Obelisk?

Syd Kelly

If it wasn't for the want of a good map, I would have found the obelisk in the first place. As it was, the monument was proving more difficult to track down than I thought. It did, after all, commemorate 'The Founder of a Nation's Unparalleled Prosperity' - a not insubstantial claim represented in Arthur Mee's *The King's England*. And not only that, the fellow had come from a small village called Heyshott in Sussex! Now I know this tome was written some sixty years ago and we have moved on since then, but it led me to wonder whether I had been missing out on something. It was then, when I discovered this eminent person also had an obelisk built to honour his achievements, that I decided this was just the excuse I needed for a bit of geographical fieldwork.

So, as this was one of those nice autumnal days that could appear in early October, I decided to investigate. Reaching for my hiking boots, car and map, although not necessarily in that order, I set out. It would certainly make for a pleasant walk on a bright, still day with the leaves still turning red and golden and I felt sure that I would encounter little difficulty in discovering this memorial. There it was on my OS map, the word: Obelisk - about one mile south of Midhurst. It was after all only a short distance off the main Chichester road. And not only that, an obelisk would surely be built where it could be seen, either on a promontory or hilltop - all very logical to my geographical mind.

Having parked my car at a place as near as I thought possible to the likely site of this notable landmark, close to Cocking Causeway, I found myself at a crossroads literally and metaphorically - a Y-junction with additional footpaths - but not an obelisk in sight. It will turn up soon enough, I conjectured.

It should perhaps be admitted here that geographers can be prone to emphasise, above all else, the necessity of possessing an accurate, readable map when undergoing an expedition 'in the field,' so it follows that there can be a tendency to blame the map when you find yourself getting 'lost' - if indeed such a condition exists. Mind you, not being able to find one's way is nothing new in deepest Sussex. As the famous political radical and raconteur William Cobbett himself discovered some 175 years earlier - Saturday, August 2nd 1823 to be precise - in contrast a very wet day by all accounts.

As he related in *Rural Rides*: 'But though I staid all day at Petworth, and though I slept here, I could get no directions how to set out to come to Singleton, where I am now. I started, therefore on the Chichester road, trusting my inquiries of the country people as I came on. By these means I got hither, down a long valley on the South Downs, which valley winds and twists amongst hills ... forming cross dells, inlets and ground in such a variety of shapes that it is impossible to describe.'

In the manner of Cobbett minus the horse, I chose to embark down a narrow, gently sloping lane that began to adopt a never-ending curve, which was determined to disappear continually from my view. But no, here across a small bridge over a stream, on a slight rise stood Dunford House, somewhat hidden from the surrounding countryside, even at this time of the year, in a sheltered wooded glade. Autumn leaves successfully camouflaged the empty car park. A notice specified no unauthorised parking. You cannot drive beyond this point, although a path leads onwards to the village of Heyshott.

Despite being in the heart of the Downland, this is not

chalk country. In this part of Sussex, it is sandstone that takes the highest ground - one such ridge holds the remains of an ancient fortification overlooking Midhurst. Down here however, the immediate area around is damp, with mixed woodland and the occasional 'babbling brook'. This was undoubtedly one of Cobbett's 'cross dells' or 'inlets.' Not that I was actually expecting an obelisk to be at the foot of a hill. At least I got something right. Perhaps this hidden landscape is not the sort of place you could have imagined would capture the nation's attention. And yet this short journey -it is just over a mile from Dunford House to West Lavington Parish Church - is one that would make national news on April 7th 1865, the day of Richard Cobden's funeral. Some 400 mourners came by train to Midhurst from London to attend the funeral, including William Gladstone who within three years would be the first Liberal Prime Minister. (The same year, incidentally, that the obelisk was built.)

In fact, the decades between 1848 and 1868 were as important as any in this neck of the woods - a time when ups and downs were as much in evidence in the social and political life of the country as the Downland landscape itself.

Whether Cobbett knew Cobden, I can only surmise. However, their paths may have crossed politically, I suppose. They were both from farming backgrounds, the former across the border in Hampshire, and both could be said to be radical personalities, in particular with regard to the changing landscape of the countryside and the farming community in particular. When Cobbett made his ride in 1823, he was already sixty or thereabouts. Richard Cobden would then have been nineteen, but from both a generational point of view and as regards their political ideas, you could say that, if their paths ever did cross politically, they would definitely have been travelling in opposite directions. Thinking about it, a sense of direction was what I seemed to be lacking that October afternoon.

Cobbett himself was very concerned about the countryside and the plight of the rural poor. In Sussex, he was more optimistic than elsewhere it would appear, remarking at one point: 'the whole of the ground, hill as well as dell is fine, most beautiful, corn land, or is covered with trees or underwood. As to St Swithin, I set him at defiance. The road was flinty, and very flinty. I rode a foot pace and got here wet to the skin. I am very glad I came this road. The corn here is all fine; all good; fine crops and no appearance of blight. There may be yet however and therefore our Government, our paternal Government so anxious to prevent over-production need not despair, not yet at any rate'.

Cobden does himself paint a less than glowing picture of his surroundings. He had spent most of his working life in the north of the country, although his family had farmed locally and he was born in the village of Heyshott in 1804. In a letter written shortly after his taking up residence at Dunford, he writes: 'There is a population here of under 300, an acreage of 2,000, one owns 1,200. All proprietors are non-resident including the vicar. There is no school, but two cottages where two illiterate old women collect a score or two of infants whilst parents are in the fields. No post office - an old man of 70 goes to collect letters at Midhurst - charges 1d each including horse collars legs of mutton empty sacks and wheelbarrows - only newspapers are two copies of Bells Weekly Messenger, a sound old Tory projectionist much patronised by drowsy farmers.'

Additionally he relates how he employs a man of 70 whose son and nephew dug and fenced for him. He believed the South Down air had something to do with the healthiness of the men who might keep a 1/4 acre garden, cut their own turf for fire, had cheap fuel from the woods and kept pigs, something Cobbett also had remarked upon.

Dunford House seemed to be exactly as it was depicted in the local newspaper when built some 150 years earlier in 1848. According to Mee, the money for the house came from a fund set up to recognise Cobden's political achievements after he had fallen into financial difficulties following his campaigning with the Anti-Corn Law League. This political

Syd Kelly archive

DUNFORD HOUSE

movement was set up in 1839 to remove tariffs on the import of grain, the infamous Corn Laws.

Meantime, I decided to revert to the top of the lane on my expedition where I continued to negotiate a meandering footpath that took me across a field towards the village of West Lavington. I scanned the skyline with increasing puzzlement and not without some mild frustration, which I hoped no one could hear, but to no avail. Being lost in thought, I managed to miss the course of the old railway line I believed Gladstone and the other mourners would have travelled on. Could every detail of this Victorian landscape have been obliterated by time? Not, at least the church, I decided.

After half an hour or so - it seemed rather longer - I was no nearer my objective. I hadn't even met anyone to ask. The countryside is so quiet these days. You scarcely meet a soul to talk to. There are plenty of people in cars though. A church must be easy to find, I reflected. But the road here was quite sunken and closed in on both sides by thick scrub and deciduous woodland of birch and beech. Only a sign saying 'Church Road' gave a clue to the proximity of the church of St Mary's.

As with the Corn Laws, the established Church itself had been coming in for much criticism in William Cobbett's age, and he had little time for the way things were. As he mused about one parish during his Sussex ride: 'The parson did not when the Return was laid before parliament in 1818 reside in the parish. Though the living is *a large living*, the parsonage house was let to *a lady and her three daughters*. What impudence a man must have to put this into a Return!' And later at Upwaltham, he relates concerning another, how: 'The church will *hold the population, but that the parsonage house would not hold him!* And why? *because it is a miserable cottage!*' (Cobbett's italics).

Had Cobbett lived a bit longer - he died in 1835 - he would have seen a transformation in church building throughout the country, as I was surprised to discover that the church at West Lavington was only built in 1850. And not only that, a new parish had been especially constructed for it. The incumbent had then promptly deferred to Rome. Such radical times in evidence here then. Cobden himself would have been resident at Dunford for only two years. Indeed, the 1840s saw the beginnings of a significant re-awakening in the fortunes of the Church of England by way of a liturgical and architectural movement, which became known as the Gothic Revival. Many new churches were built, mostly in towns and cities, but West Lavington was one such new Church, built to a specified design by an influential architect called William Butterfield. By thus creating places of worship more akin to pre-Reformation designs, they intended to instill more reverence to worship, which to agree with Cobbett, had become somewhat dissipated. Buildings such as that at West Lavington gave physical shape to such ideals. It might be argued nowadays, I suppose, that such campaigning in the Anglican Church would be interpreted as exhibiting a kind of 'religious correctness'.

RICHARD COBDEN (1865)
replica by Giuseppe Fagnani of his own work (1860-61)

those causes that united country and town, farmers and industrial workers - against the land-owning gentry in particular.

Here we might witness both Cobbett and Cobden in agreement. At a time when Cobbett rode and Cobden proclaimed, these laws were increasingly perceived by many as unfair. They benefited essentially those land-owners, not exactly beloved by Cobbett, who were naturally a formidable political lobby - that is if they weren't the politicians themselves. In Sussex, Cobbett remained somewhat speculative: 'I suppose that every inch of land that I came through this morning belongs either to the Duke of Richmond, or to Lord Egremont. No harm in that if those who till the land have *fair play*'.

For the poverty to be observed in the countryside, he largely blamed unscrupulous landlords: 'There is one farmer, in the North of Hampshire, who has nearly eight thousand acres of land in his hands... is it any wonder that paupers increase?' In another passage he remarked: 'The wise men of the newspapers are for a repeal of the Corn Laws. With all my heart, I will join any body in a petition for their repeal.' Thus wrote Cobbett in 1825.

So the rage against the Corn Laws did indeed unite Cobbett and Cobden for a time. Still, I was no nearer finding my obelisk. I felt a Cobbett-like diatribe coming on about the poor quality of signposts in the countryside. I am led to relate, in the manner of one of his asides, how my dictionary gives a definition of the word 'obelisk' as meaning a mark used in ancient manuscript to signify a 'spurious', 'corrupt', or 'doubtful' word or passage*

Hmm . . . Perhaps, I mused, it was no longer there and this was all a waste of a journey. The repeal of the Corn Laws in 1846 might be said to represent a major turning point in British political history, sowing the seeds of a new political creed which would ultimately transform political life in Britain. In point of fact, on its own, the repeal did little to alter

*It is also a dagger, a symbol used for footnotes.

actual corn prices and the duty did not entirely disappear. Meanwhile, much of the revenue due to the Government was replaced by the introduction of income tax, which of course we accept quite naturally today . . . So it is indeed memorable for this aspect of fiscal policy alone.

It might even with more emphasis be said to confirm the political stature of a newly-establishing manufacturing and mercantile culture of which Cobden was a central participant. In this sense, he was paving the way for the career politicians so familiar in our political life today, eulogising as they do the benefits of global, free market economies. The ruling hegemony of the land-owning classes was permanently in retreat. The Empire was on its way.

Cobden was indeed looking to the future. For although he had been born into a farming community, by becoming an industrialist/entrepreneur he was bound to perceive the Corn Laws as a hindrance to his business affairs. By keeping the price of bread artificially high, they had become a source of contention for workers, thereby putting pressure on wages and consequently reducing profits. They also acted to increase the price of other goods, such as the cotton cloth Cobden wished to sell abroad. All this sounds quite familiar today.

So was he merely showing self-interest? Certainly, it would appear so from his stance on the Ten Hours Bill which restricted, one year after the successful repeal, the working hours of women and children in factories. Interestingly, he voted against this. In reality it meant that factories had to stop working for some part of the day, as men could not realistically carry on alone. No obelisk would commemorate this I am afraid.

How much of a political enemy here would Cobbett then have been: 'Talk of serfs', he wrote. 'Are there any of these, or did feudal times ever see any of them so debased so absolutely slaves as the poor creatures who in the enlightened North are compelled to work fourteen hours in a day in a heat of eighty-four degrees; and who are liable to punishment for looking out at a window of the factory.' But then Cobden could be said to show more consistency than Cobbett. A modern biographer has stated: 'He argued that the only practical way to reduce hours without reducing wages was a policy of Free Trade which would lead to increased production and higher wages. Notwithstanding all the evidence to the contrary produced by the Short Time Committees, he insisted that the workers did not want shorter hours.'

Following his victory in the Corn Law campaign, Cobden became a vigorous campaigner for the ideal of Free Trade. One of his major achievements was a Trade Treaty with France in 1860 which reduced French duties on coal and on most manufacture goods not exceeding 30 per cent. In return Britain lowered duties on French wines and brandy. The value of trade doubled between 1859 and 1869 as a result. Indeed, Cobden deplored the notion of Government intervention in foreign affairs and hence was against Britain's participation in the Crimean War. Of course, this might be seen as taking a humanitarian stance in contrast to the factory legislation above. As he recommended in another paper on Russia, there should be: 'as little intercourse as possible between Governments, as much connection as possible between the nations of the world. I see in the Free Trade principle that which shall act on the moral world as the principle of gravitation in the Universe - drawing men together, thrusting aside the antagonism of race and creed and language and uniting us in the bonds of eternal peace.'

Cobden, however, could even remain far-sighted when he predicted the following scenario in writing: 'the desire and the motivation for large and mighty armies... for those materials used for the destruction of life and the desolation of the rewards of labour will die away.' In such ways Cobden represents the future: individualism, free market competition, a libertarian trumpeting non-government interference. This also sounds familiar. Well, I could remind myself, it was only a short journey I was making that day after all.

I began to feel decidedly chilly. As the early October dusk approached, I decided to give in to the inevitable and return home. A woman clearing some garden rubbish had directed me to the location of the obelisk from the church. The spot she described seemed to suggest where I had come from. Impossible. Reaching the car, I wandered around in a small circle. There was a hedge where I had parked. I looked over. There was the obelisk, plain to see, very plain, in fact grey and stolid, and bearing the inscription:

FREE TRADE
PEACE AND GOOD WILL
AMONG NATIONS

and to one side in small letters, 'carved by Mr. James Grist, stonemason of Midhurst, on land provided by Mr. Henry Court in 1868, 34 feet high and 70 feet above the turnpike road'. How could I have missed it?

Free trade-among nations, it said. If anything has dominated our lives in the twentieth century, it has been the rise of Nation States. Interestingly, Italy had just been unified at the time of Cobden's death and Germany was to follow in 1871. The twentieth century has undoubtedly been one of rampant Nationalism, an anathema to the establishment of Free Trade. Protectionism has ruled. The point is perhaps to note how Free Trade is invariably argued in the context of the Nation State. But are we now beginning to see the decline of this? Do

OBELISK
WEST LAVINGTON

Syd Kelly archive

multi-national companies rule? Are Cobden's ideas to be vindicated after all?

Not that there aren't any international organisations: the United Nations, the IMF, the World Bank for example. Would Cobden have approved? Perhaps not. In Cobden's view the world would have been 'not a society of States but of peoples'. Perhaps this is no more realistic than the Gothic Revival in the Church or the paternal views of Cobbett.

Nowadays would Cobden be seen, not as a disinterested Internationalist, but as a British economic nationalist, perpetuating Free Trade in a world economic system? Perhaps. Geographers, it must be said, like to believe they present a balanced, all-inclusive view of these matters.

Meantime, transformations in society - cultural, religious, economic - have continued to this day. But just as importantly, underlying philosophies ebb and flow as well.

From a geographer's point of view this is the important issue. Current developments in the global market would seem to suggest that forces establishing the credentials for Free Trade are still on-going. The free flow of money, connected to major currency speculation for example, only recently threatened loss of economic control as the major world governments had to intervene to stave off fears of global 'meltdown'. So is Free Trade really possible? And if so, can it be free for all? As an economic ideal, it certainly seems to have survived, whilst the hopes of Cobbett by contrast, seem to have vanished. The liberal views of Cobden and the growth of the business class has all but eclipsed that of the old landed gentry and aristocracy, except perhaps in the House of Lords. But even for them, how long?

One of the striking aspects of the obelisk, which I have not commented on, is that it proclaims: peace and goodwill. The existence of peace and goodwill throughout the world has, alas, still to be negotiated. Nations themselves remain both the barrier and the stimulus to much of this, including Free Trade. They are, by definition, organized groups of peoples and territories independent of other peoples and territories.

They each inevitably have their own agendas. To recognise this is to accept difference.

So here we go again, circling round and round with seemingly diametrically opposed world-views and maybe not getting very far. Differences can lead to conflicts of interest. Conflicts of interest can lead to protectionism in trade as a means of self-determination and survival. Peace and Good Will are left to pick up the pieces. Of course the obelisk of Egyptian architecture is noted for its solidity, its earthing, grounded effect - a firm base more symbolically relevant than its tapering spire. Coventry Patmore, a Victorian poet, gave expression to this when he wrote that: 'Egyptian architecture exhibited not only power but the permanence of power. The pyramid is secure against the injuries of time - the shape of a mountain - nature's own architecture - suggests a heap of masonry thrown down by the Almighty. Its shape, a passive symbol of gravity, indicates weight unrelieved by construction: the simplest architectural expression of mere ponderosity. The obelisk is a sort of shorthand expression of the same idea, that is, the idea of weight in the abstract.'

So where are we now? The obelisk, the railway, and the church had been hidden from my view and are we anywhere nearer finding wealth in Free Trade or Faith in Christ? One hundred and fifty years after Marx's famous manifesto, Communism too is supposedly in retreat. Only the obelisk itself, as an image of unrelieved weight, in a curious way seeks to defy eternity.

The physical landscape, what we observe, is constantly changing, but other more hidden landscapes are changing too, that is if we can discover them. Often they remain obscured from view - like the obelisk was for me that day. At least I could easily visit it again. I had my car. I couldn't have got there otherwise, with little public transport to speak of. Mobility changes everything. For one thing, increased mobility seems to have led to greater insecurity. Who can be sure what might happen, when outsiders come unnoticed from afar? Nowadays even the Church is locked.

Protectionism rules here also.

One worthy traveller, an American, had made the most recent entry in the church visitors' book. Apparently he came from a small town in Illinois, USA, called Cobden, named after the great man himself. Had the Church itself impressed this visitor? It made me wonder.

Still, I wouldn't need a map the next time. Perhaps it is having the right map that counts. Or maybe there never is one map that can tell us everything we need to know, although I suppose there are still some who might think otherwise.

ALFRED, LORD TENNYSON
watercolour by William Henry Margetson (1891)
after a photograph by Herbert Barraud (1882)

THIRTEEN

CHASING THE LIGHT: A ROLL OF FILM IN THE CUCKMERE VALLEY

Chris Waters

A walk from Michelham Priory along the Weald Way, to Cuckmere Haven
Sunday 11 April 1999

for Sandra

I

7.00 am wide angle, f11 @ 250
Michelham Priory /early dew - sun rising about the Gate Tower catching
young silver birch leaves/light wind flaking the surface of the moat/how
to capture birdsong?

II

close-upf8 @ 125
Just on the fringes of Michelham - skirting Mill Wood/bunches of pale
primroses under dark-gloss holly in the hedges.

III

7.07am wide-angle f16 @ 125
Outskirts of Michelham/low sun, still/long-tapering shadows - trees and
me - converging across the furrows of a coarse-ploughed field/topshine
where the share has sliced then turned the earth.

IV

7.21 am zoom f11 @ 250
The pond by Winham Coppice /calm water steaming easy in the
sun/'Private water'/deep trees upside down, and air-rings, vanishing.

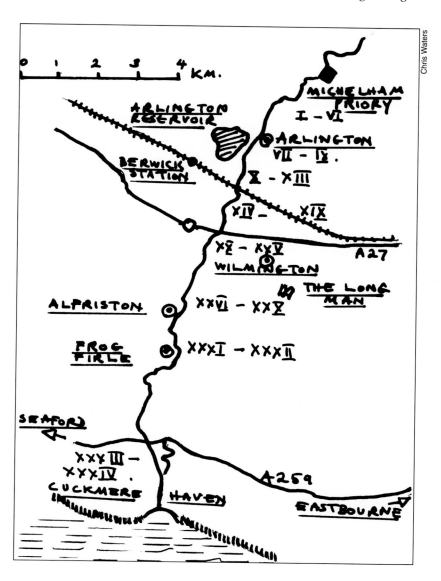

Chris Waters

MICHELHAM PRIORY TO CUCKMERE HAVEN

V

wide-angle, f16 @ 125
Almost-silent field near Raylands Farm, south of Michelham/still-dew-wet/in the far corner a blackened tree by a gate/a huddle of sheep with the light just arcing across their backs.

VI

7.44 long shot f11 @ 500
South of Raylands Farm, looking SW across the concealed river Cuckmere/first glimpse of Arlington Reservoir - a pale-blue sword of light/in the distance, Firle Beacon - big shoulders the colour of elephant hide.

VII

7.46 standard f11 @ 250
Arlington Church - squat, hipped red roof, and little hexagonal, conical spire/framed, mirrored (mocked?) by a rusty pylon.

VIII

7.48 standard f11 @ 250
By the Church/double barns, sturdy with worn, warm pink brick and hipped tiled roofs/ridge-beams sagging/I think of Edward Thomas.

IX

7.55 close-up f8 @ 125
The Churchyard/a sun-caught tomb - toblerone shaped/ivy, lichens, moss, dandelions and nettles - and barley twist iron railings - like a bedstead/'To the Memory of Ruth, wife of John Page of Ringmer, aged 37. . . '

X

8.05 standard f16 @ 125
Sun over my shoulder/standing on a high bank by the inert Cuckmere/arched metal footbridge/then a water shimmer as the wind shifts.

XI

8.10 wide angle f16 @ 250
(sound of Berwick train in the distance) - Stapley's - huddled barns and garden walls/a corrugated lean-to/stacked logs catching the light, and a mound of picked flints, and three doves, drinking at an old white metal bowl.

XXXIII

12.20 wide angle f16 @ 250
On the penultimate, straight-cut, stretch of the Cuckmere/clouds fuller, blue-grey now/bruised-leather glance of light from a crow's wing as it tilts across the field.

XXXIV

1.00 pm wide angle f16 @ 500
On the public footpath, Seaford Head Nature Reserve/wide open estuary/courses of old creeks and rivulets, pock-marked with hoof holes/skittering flies snapped by diving birds/buff-stone Charolais bull grazing squarely - light ridging his flanks and hump.

XXXV

1.30 pm wide angle f16 @ 500
The Edge: Chyngton/wide opening into light, but the sea layered in grape, slate and turquoise/'Belle Tout' lighthouse shadow-striped in the distance/low-tide shingle sweeping round to the first of the Seven Sisters - brides or spinsters, virgins or widows?/chalk like worried lace/I think of Miss Havisham.

XXXVI

Finis: I turn inland and face the beginning of the day, re-wound on this roll of film, and head homeward, wondering how it will print.

FOURTEEN

Philip Hughes: FLINT LINE IN THE CLIFF TO THE EAST OF BIRLING
GAP (DETAIL - 22 OCT. 88)

This drawing, on recycled paper and heightened with colour, is
taken from *Patterns in the Landscape: The Notebooks of Philip Hughes*
(Thames and Hudson, 1998), a collection of work from the past ten
years: the volume features landscapes in Sussex, Wiltshire, and
Dorset, as well as in France, Australia, the States, Iceland, Ireland,
Scotland, and Wales. Writing about his drawing, Philip Hughes
comments that it was the drawing of the Sussex cliff that led to an
interest in 'the strata of landscape' and to a preoccupation in many
other drawings with rock strata.

Flint is a common building material along the southern slopes of
the South Downs, and for travellers across the county, especially
from north to south (and vice-versa) it can be engaging to note the
transition from brick to flint and back to brick. Flints for building
are still being produced in Sussex, at the Duncton chalk quarry
south of Petworth, for example - see Brian Dawson, *Flint Buildings
in West Sussex* (West Sussex County Council, 1998)

FIFTEEN

Reshaped by the Sea:
S.T. Coleridge and Littlehampton

John Wyatt

In Sussex in 1817, two careers crossed. One was the path of Samuel Taylor Coleridge, poet, philosopher and medically dependant dreamer, and the other the longer slower trajectory of a small town, then spelt (by those who could) Little Hampton.[*]

Every town changes in time, sometimes so much speedier than the geography of the out-of-town landscape with the slow beat of its geological clock. Towns are so interfused by our own shorter life stories that we are always tempted to describe urban landscapes in terms of growth, maturity, and decline but, even reading from the narrative of the full human life, the analogy does not hold up. A town's life is not like our own. Our human curve of growth and decline is just simpler - up and down. A town seems to flourish, grow and then diminish, perhaps pause, and then grow again. Yet a settlement is not exempt from death, although we with our Western industrialized experience think that urban sites are immortal, an unstoppable growth of the urban, weakly contained by green belts. Towns can also diminish and even disappear. In 1817, along the West Sussex coast there was ample evidence of settlement extinction. Under the Channel are drowned villages, inhabited within the eighteenth and nineteenth centuries' living memory - Middleton to the west,

*See p. 130

parts of Atherington, Cudlowe and its woods south of Climping. Littlehampton itself had suffered from the shifting sands of natural coastal and river change. The River Arun inexorably and rapidly (in a geological time-scale) was steadily wearing away the South Downs, daily discharging its milky load of erosion into the Channel. The Channel itself, in a twice-daily reciprocation, flowed up the mouths of the Arun and deposited its sand and gravel on the surrounding levels and marshes. 'Mouths' of the Arun is a good metaphor for the years before Reorganising Enlightened Man did anything about it, for Little Hampton's river entered the sea by a number of channels, spilling slowly out into a delta of streams between clay islets.* In times of high tides, or when the inland rains eventually discharged their turbid silt the fields were flooded for miles.

In earlier days (or at least 'earlier' in the human historical sense) the coastline had been firm enough to attract a small but economically useful trade so the small village had some profit from Channel commerce. It even had a small part in national history. William Rufus landed here in 1097. In 1139, Princess Matilda, daughter of Henry I, landed at Little Hampton with 140 knights, in order to challenge King Stephen's right to the English throne. She progressed only as far as Arundel, negotiated a diplomatic solution instead of a war and departed in peace. Four centuries or so later, a Dunkirk ship was successfully boarded from a ship out of Little Hampton and a valuable painting of Saint Ursula was taken and sent to the Star Chamber. Silt, shingle, and muddy flood in the following two centuries had inexorably diminished the town and it sank back to the status of a village amongst the marshes with small 'upland' levels a few feet above flooding as the base for Church, farm and cottages.

*Readers of the history of Littlehampton (and here I use the new way of spelling) must be grateful for the work of H. J. F. Thompson who published interesting monographs about the history of the town, as well as collecting oral history and fascinating prints and photographs. The booklets are in local libraries (e.g. *Littlehampton Long Ago*, published by J. F. Ltd, Bognor Regis, c. 1985). I acknowledge my debt to Thompson's assiduous collecting.

The small rise of land at the junction of East Street and Church Street at the end of what is now the pedestrianised High Street is the main remnant of the diminished mid-life of Little Hampton. The only continuously passable road into the town was from Angmering in the east and the Arun could only be crossed by carts at Arundel. The inhabitants were mocked by snootier Arundel people as being sickly marsh dwellers - that is until a new life began with Improvement.

The essential economic ingredient, as many places in the kingdom were discovering in the early eighteenth century was Landed Money. In the Fens, the Duke of Bedford provided the necessary. In Little Hampton, the major landowner was the Duke of Norfolk, settled at Arundel Castle and London for generations and, like many of his peers, beginning to be interested in Changing and Tidying, the refined art of Improvement. In 1732, he successfully petitioned Parliament for authority to reorganize errant Nature. The River Arun was put under the new discipline of engineers. A very successful scheme of straightening the lazy river was accomplished with piers protecting vessels entering the single channel harbour mouth, although there were permanent problems of creeping sand bars. Little Hampton as a port had arrived. More significant still for the noble Duke entrepreneur, the river was now fully navigable to Arundel and eventually linked with the canal system from the west and to the north. Little Hampton began to awaken to what we have called the Industrial Revolution, but contemporaries settled for the word 'prosperity'.

The first phase of the European War of the end of the century and the beginning of the next saw considerable growth in wartime industry. Large boats including a man of war of 546 tons were built at yards next to what is now Town Quay. The port became a regular staging post for coastal traffic bringing coals (from Newcastle!) and other heavy imports for transferring up river and collecting timber and farm products from the hinterland. Continental trade was hindered by the

visit a travel guide for Brighton, Worthing, Bognor and Little Hampton had described the resort in this way:

'The purity of the sea air, cheapness, and retirement, seem to be the principal recommendations of this place, which is certainly well adapted for family parties, whose enjoyments begin and end in their own circle. Such indeed will find comfort and amusement anywhere, even at home which is so much dreaded by the unhappy and the dissipated, and such will find Little Hampton more congenial to their taste than the resorts of wealth and grandeur' (*Bognor, Arundel, and Little Hampton Guide,* Chichester, 1828).

Plainly this was no Brighton, rather a place for 'people with moderate tastes'. Whether this description quite fitted Coleridge can be argued, but there is no doubt that as a place of retreat from anxiety, this was well suited. We know that the resort had been thought to be of value for one anxious parent to take her errant son's mind off the attractions of London. He was a young man fully capable of realising the potential of London's excitement and vices. George Gordon, Lord Byron, at seventeen on his first vacation from Cambridge was persuaded by his mother to take a seaside holiday with Cambridge friends, the Longs. After a stop at Worthing, they put up at the Dolphin Inn, at that time a coaching house for the London trade and already acquiring the reputation for protecting smugglers. The site and the pub name remain attached to a modern inn at the corner of Surrey Street and High Street. Byron's stay is unremarkable except for a river escapade. The straightened Arun was not only fully tidal, its flow and ebb were very fast. An Admiralty chart of 1830 notes that there was a rise and fall of around sixteen feet at times of ordinary spring tides. 'The flood', Lieutenant Barnett of the Survey notes, 'runs in with high velocity until one hour after high water, but immediately outside the Eastern Pier Head from half flood to half ebb it sets strong to the westward.' In this treacherous stream Byron and his young friends swam and recorded that they were swept out by the current. But for the fact that the young milord was a powerful swimmer, Little

Hampton might have achieved notoriety as the last appearance of a potential great poet. Whether Coleridge knew that the stream which courses through the harbour, darkly flowing in its inland pilgrimage and grey with chalk scouring its way out to sea, had only ten years before threatened the future of Byron is not known. If Coleridge himself swam - and it is likely he did if we take seriously his progress in taking to the sea bathing fashion in Hampshire and in subsequent years at Ramsgate - he would have used the bathing machines hauled into the edge of the sea in front of the Common which lies before the South (Beach)Terrace.

Urban geographers have provided at least one vibrant neologism for those who breathe more rapidly at language which evokes the past. It is the notion of the 'cadastre', the preexisting pattern of settlement still possible to perceive, like ghostly vestiges, beneath an urban cover (see Morris, E.A.J., *History of Urban Form before the Industrial Revolution*, 1994). There are traces of old field boundaries, dips and ridges of past workings of the land, and of former streams still visible for the initiated below Littehampton's modern surfaces. Perhaps the busy small town life held memories for Coleridge, mental cadastres of his hectic early manhood, remote enough to observe without anxiety. The harbour was guarded by a small platoon of soldiers with two officers in charge, a remnant of the anxiety of the defence of the realm of recent war years. Their cannon was fired ceremoniously on Sundays. Their barracks, with the noises of military life, were close, but not too close to the new smart terrace for the convalescents and the quiet families on holiday. Perhaps there were memories of his own strange military episode of 1791 as Dragoon S. T. Comberbach. There was sufficient stir in the harbour of the relatively new town by the river to chime with the poet's experience of the sea and with his fascination with ships. The bowsprits of large vessels, some being prepared for

The Terrace, Littlehampton.

the West Indian trade, overhung the walkways alongside Town Quay. Competition for the dues payable to pilots guiding ships into the tricky harbour was fierce. The shouts of entrepreneurial 'hufflers' or 'hovellers', boatmen who earned a living by taking small supplies to ships lying out in the Channel or by ferrying hopeful pilots, would be heard along the small quaysides. Northern voices joined the tumult, as ships from Northumberland and Yorkshire unloaded onto craft that could be sailed up river. The sounds of a harbour at work would have reminded this wandering poet of the small, but busy Somerset port of Watchet, near Nether Stowey, where, it was said, the idea of the Ancient Mariner emerged.

Coleridge was not, however, on a collecting expedition for material for poetry. He had commissioned work enough with the 'Introduction to the Encyclopaedia' for Rest Fenner, as well as with assembling the mass of information he always required for a new series of public lectures that winter. More to the point, he was in Little Hampton for reasons of health like many others at that time. His first letters from his retreat reveal that again the stress and the opiate were taking a toll on his physical frame. Most agonising for him, next to the nightmares, was a familiar enemy, his digestive chaos. Opium addiction can engender acute constipation, although at times the opposite symptoms can occur dramatically. Coleridge had suffered from these acute digestive irritations at various junctures of his life, notably on his journey by sea from Malta in 1806. Although they were a repeated feature of his life, they were a frightening affliction, for even the smallest signs reminded him of the terrible journey from Malta when he was in unforgettable pain. Not that he ever kept these fears or descriptions of detailed physical effects to himself. He described the symptoms in a letter to John Murray on the 28 September: 'a state of terror and extreme despondency with regard to everything... the cause I have reason to believe is some slight stricture in the higher bowel.' His 'hastening to the sea coast' did not, immediately reduce the sensations, but strong 'Calomel Doses for several days' effected 'violent removal' of a something . . . just below the pit of my stomach. Typically he uses the image of the nightmare and the state of sleep to explain the relief: 'This occurred early yester morning - and if you can imagine what it would be to awake in health out of a painful Dream, you will have a tolerable notion of my present state of mind. There is only one more guarded reference to ill health. Writing to James Gillman on 29 October he says, 'My health is in some respects improved' (Griggs, letters 1078, 1079). Little Hampton with its regular routines, the careful nursing of Ann Gillman (we have no knowledge of the whereabouts of the Gillman children on this holiday), the regular exercise of walking by the sea, and the absence of London gossip about reviews of his work seemed to have effected a convalescence.

Convalescence was Little Hampton's business. As well as being a place of bulk transhipment, the town had begun to participate in a health industry which was beginning to make its mark on the human geography of the British Isles. First were the spa town developments, sometimes linked with *bon ton* as at Bath, but more mundanely elsewhere with the quest for healing waters in places as widely distributed as Scarborough, Llandrindod, Lincoln, Leamington, Epsom, and Tonbridge. Then there was the direction of the public's attention by medical practitioners (qualified or unqualified) to the advantages of sea bathing. The end of the eighteenth century saw the rapid development of 'watering places', equipped with bathing machines, bathing attendants, and brine baths. In 1781, William Cowper writes of them:

> Your prudent grand-mammas, ye modern belles,
> Content with Bristol, Bath and Tunbridge wells,
> When health requir'd it would consent to roam,
> Else more attached to pleasures found at home,
> But now alike, gay widow, virgin, wife,
> Ingenious to diversify dull life,
> In coaches, chaises, caravans, and hays,
> Fly to the coast for daily, nightly joys
> (William Cowper, from 'Retirement').

The sea side resorts were often quieter small places, reasonably close to London positioned on the milder coast of the country. Again there was a touch of royal ëbon toní at Brighton, but less ambitious, though nevertheless smart settlements were popular at Eastbourne, Worthing, Bognor, and Little Hampton.

In the last case it is possible to identify the medical authority who encouraged the town with the commendation : 'the most healthy aspect on the Sussex coast'. This was the well-known Doctor John Abernethy (1764-1831) known to Coleridge because of his methods of treating addiction and acquainted at least in medical argument with Dr Gillman about their common areas of interest. Coleridge indeed assisted Gillman in assembling an argument about the essential nature of living things (a subject close to the poet's interests in German *Naturphilosophie*), a topic also addressed by Abernethy. Doctor Abernethy is recorded by oral tradition as having stayed at the George Inn in Little Hampton. A story was generated that he gave not only his usual prescription biscuits but also very brusque advice to a wealthy lady about over-eating. His own master theory was that the human system was all linked to the digestive organs. Therefore his treatments were abstinence and purgatives. It is easy to see why Coleridge had dreaded going under his care in 1808! Evidently Abernethy did more than stay at the small inn, for in an 1822 sketch book by the artist, William Clift,[*] there is a drawing of the South Terrace (Beach Terrace) with the easternmost house in the terrace house labelled as 'MrsAbernethy's'. Next door is identified as that of another doctor, Warburton. Clift's sketch also shows that, far from being a drab row of Georgian houses, the Terrace had many attractive features, with differently coloured doors and window frames. Little Hampton was not a spa but its new economy was built on restoring health.

One of the seekers after renewal in the autumn of 1817 was a visitor who was to become a close friend of Coleridge. Little Hampton provided the locale for their first meeting. The Reverend Henry Cary was a scholar, with what at the time seemed an insignificant piece of translation of a very significant world-renowned figure, Dante Alighieri. Cary's upbringing was not unusual for a member of a growing group of intelligentsia interested in Italian culture who were sought, after a slow start, by major publishers. He was born in 1772, and spent his childhood in Staffordshire, and then attended Rugby School until his health caused his parents to withdraw him. He quickly showed promise with poetry in his own language as well as with classical and modern tongues.

---

[*]William Clift's sketches are in Littlehampton Museum. Clift (1775 -1849) also had medical connections. He was illustrator assistant to John Hunter, the famous anatomist, recording the major collections of human and fossils collected by Hunter. After Hunter's death, Clift became keeper of the collection.

Always a quiet and retiring man (Charles Lamb described Cary as a man of 'almost extreme modesty and sensibility'), he nevertheless made friends with a range of intellectuals who led cultured life in the provinces at the end of the eighteenth century. Prominent among them was the author, Anna Seward, through whom Cary met William Hayley of Eartham, Sussex. Indeed, during his stay in Little Hampton in 1817 and 1818, Cary visited the by now ageing and tiring old literary entrepreneur who had been of assistance to many artists, including William Blake and William Cowper nearly twenty years before. Hayley had retired to his new Turret House home at Felpham, now so easily reached from modern Littlehampton, but in 1817 requiring either a long ride round to Arundel and then a southward trek or a shorter route via a ferryman and a quiet road west via Climping.

Cary's translation of Dante was well known to Hayley. Indeed, he was himself engaged on a translation of the master. Fortunately, Cary's translation is the one that is remembered, although it was not seen to be so important by the booksellers on first publication in 1812. Coleridge had much to do with encouraging London publishers to accept a larger print run for a second very successful edition, which became the major nineteenth-century English version and is still published today. That is to move ahead beyond this Little Hampton story.

Little Hampton had again been chosen for a cure. Cary suffered from disabling bouts of deep anxiety. The first appears to have followed a family bereavement. Intermittent depressions caused him to seek medical guidance in London where he held a parson's living (in Chiswick). Ill health was sufficiently grave to make him abandon his writing for stretches of two or three years. Somehow he was always able to start again after a disabling pause. In 1817, the signs were not good for Cary's state of mind. His youngest daughter had recently died of consumption and the following spring, his youngest son, Francis, became ill with worryingly familiar symptoms, It was then that the Cary's decided to seek recovery on the south coast. They stayed briefly at Worthing and then moved to Little Hampton's Beach Terrace. As well as visiting his old mentor, Hayley in Felpham, Cary, no doubt educating his son, also visited, like any modern Sussex tourist, Amberley Castle, and the excavations of the Roman Villa at Bignor. Mrs Cary was heavily pregnant when Coleridge met her husband, for, in November 1817, when Coleridge was either ready to leave or had already left for London, a son, Richard was born in Little Hampton.

The meeting between the two different labourers in the harvest of poetry is worth recording in the way it was told by Cary's son, Henry, then a boy of thirteen. He was the cause of their coming together. Henry Cary junior recorded years later that his father had recognized Coleridge walking at Little Hampton, but had been too shy to make himself known to the poet. He had already acknowledged Coleridge's leadership in criticism, for, in the introductory preface to the translation of Dante, Carey had referred to Coleridge in this way: 'I do not regard those hours as the least happy of my life, during which, (to use the eloquent language of Mr Coleridge) "my individual recollections have been suspended, and lulled to sleep, amid the music of holier thoughts".' The son's account also reveals something of the intensity of the upbringing of bright young boys by their earnest fathers at this time. He had been learning Greek and Latin with his father and in this winter period had completed Homer's *Iliad* and was pursuing the *Odyssey*: 'After a morning's toil over Greek and Latin composition it was our custom to walk on the sands and read Homer aloud, a practice adopted for the sake of the sea breezes, and not a little, I believe, in order that the pupil might learn *"ore rotundo"*, having to raise his voice above the noises of the sea that was breaking at our feet. For several consecutive days, Coleridge crossed us in our walk. The sound of the Greek and especially the expressive countenance of the tutor, attracted his notice; so one day, as we met, he placed himself directly in my father's way and thus accosted him: "Sir, yours is a face I should know, I am Samuel Taylor Coleridge".' (King, R.W., *The Translator of Dante, Work and Friendships of Henry Francis Cary: 1772-1844*, 1925, p. 111)

This is a striking way of making oneself known, almost on a par with other great greetings of the nineteenth century (Dr Livingstone . . . . !). Its effect was to encourage a friendship which started immediately with Coleridge in one of his bravura moods. The excited poet walked with them to the house which the Carys had rented, talking all the time. Did Coleridge walk in his typical wandering fashion, as William Hazlitt had so amazingly noted twenty years before, crossing and recrossing his companion's path and discoursing all the while? We do know that Coleridge was in impressive form. Young Henry says it 'could not be called talking or conversing'. He waxed long about Homer, borrowed Cary's copy of the Dante translation, returned it next morning, and astounded his new friends with his ability to repeat whole pages from memory together with the original Italian.

Cary was recalled to London in October 1817, although he obviously returned to Little Hampton for family duties, perhaps after Coleridge had returned to Highgate. Cary's reputation grew aided by the introductions Coleridge was able to make almost immediately on his own return to the centre of things. In his public lecture in January, 1818, for instance, Coleridge referred eloquently to the virtues of Cary's *Dante*. New mutual frienships were built, such as with Charles Lamb and Henry Crabb Robinson. Cary, son and father never forgot their meeting on the shore.

Coleridge made one other lasting friendship in Little Hampton. This was with C. A. Tulk, a man of affairs who later became a Member of Parliament. More to Coleridge's intellectual point, Tulk was a Swedenborgian. This mystical philosophical movement, which a little earlier had interested William Blake, was a rich source of metaphysical nourishment to the temporary sage of Little Hampton. We have a clue when and where Coleridge met the intellectual politician. Coleridge records in correspondence meeting Tulk in the Reading Room, which we can conjecture was the circulating library near the *New Inn* at the western end of the Beach Terrace. The inn is there now, but renewed, retaining only its name. The Reading Room has long gone.

We can also surmise where Tulk lodged. The poet wrote a letter to Tulk dated September 1817 in which he excuses the late delivery of the messages in it, because 'I was just three quarters of an hour too late when I called at number 6'. Presumably this is Number 6, Beach Terrace (Griggs, letter 1174; see also Richard Holmes, *Darker Reflections*, 1998, p. 459). Strangely enough, Coleridge did not send the letter to his new friend until after his return to Highgate, the reason being that he did not want Tulk to have to pay the postage. In that period, unless you had a privileged 'frank' for postage (say from an M.P.), the receiver paid the cost. It was not a light missive and contained a long argument about the nature of God, accompanied by an equally long appendix explaining more abstruse points mentioned in the substantive argument. To Coleridge this was 'a very, very rude and fragmentary demonstration of the Objective Pole or the science of the construction of Nature'. Coleridge enjoyed the company of Tulk's family as he was to enjoy the companionship of the Carys a few weeks later. During the brief crossing of ways in Little Hampton he obviously felt entranced by both Tulk and his wife. He was to commend Tulk to Hugh J. Rose as 'A Gentleman of Fortune, a man of more than ordinary talent and more than ordinary Erudition'. Mrs Tulk achieved even greater praise : 'The Mother of the boys is - I am tempted to say the loveliest woman in countenance, manner and nature that I have ever seen'. What Tulk contributed to the resting Coleridge then and to the reinvigorated philosopher in London later was an opportunity for deep digging into important matters, that is important to Coleridge and Tulk, not primarily the affairs of the day, the harsh government reactions to the post-war protest movements and to the primitive trades unions, but the essential nature of the human mind and the nature of the spirit. There is some indication

succession crisis to the throne was potentially risk-creating, but also the Princess had been a favourite visitor to the area. She had enjoyed holidays at Sir Richard Hotham's Dome at Bognor and had been a very accepted and popular visitor to the social gatherings in the neighbourhood.

Certainly, Little Hampton steadily grew, as did most of England's resorts, with the additional advantage of what appeared to be a port linked with the industrial growth of a rich agricultural region. The railway came in mid-century and, more than its facility to take and send goods, it seized the opportunity to enlarge a more profitable, longer lasting trade, the people trade. Until the Second World War, there was no pause in the development of the seaside resort of what became known as (one word) Littlehampton, so well aligned for day trippers, charabanc excursions, South London family weeks at the briny, and even a little out-of-season tripping as well. Eventually a fair ground owner named Butlin built a popular amusement funfair on the site of the mound where the Battery had tried to defend Little Hampton against the French - a good example of swords and ploughshares. The Oyster Pond became democratic - a boating lake. New housing estates developed within the town boundary and crept along the coast into small villages like East Preston, Angmering, and Ferring, until, by 1960, there were few green gaps between the clusters of bungalows. More prosperous new estates of larger houses appeared along the leafy roads and around small village nuclei along the coastal fringe.

At a very early stage in Victoria's reign, the gap in the settlement pattern between the old town with its harbour and the select South Terrace had begun to fill. With increasing river trade, the east bank was raised and drained, new industries constructed (some with names that persist in Littlehampton's directories today), and row after row of small houses, many for holiday accommodation each equipped with that new, formidable economic entity, the seaside landlady, were built, until the town became one complete, unarticulated mass of housing. Health still provided a spring for trade. In the twentieth century, Convalescent Homes flourished, but in recent times they gave way to the new phase of urban property, the nursing home adaptations of larger houses, aspects of the late twentieth-century health industry. The new future of Littlehampton was again reshaped as a place to escape one's toiling past or the city stresses, particularly of South London. Retirement, as a new life phase, assisted the town to grow.

But what of the other economy, the expected surge of industry and trade because of the harbour? Although for a long time the river attracted ocean and Channel traffic, and, when the railway came, there was a surge in optimism about the opportunities for even greater industrial growth, the die was cast against major development owing to the old inflexibility of geography, the shape of the river mouth. Cross-Channel ships became larger; world-wide shipping sought large ports. The decision by the railway company to route its cross-channel passenger ferry business to Newhaven was crucial in determining that Littlehampton would not flourish as a major Channel port.

The town continued to have its artistic moments. John Constable, visiting Arundel, painted the port in 1835. Strangely enough, its two most distinguished literary visitors in the next hundred years, like Byron and Cary before them, both resided briefly at Worthing before taking up summer accommodation at Littlehampton. George Eliot stayed at the Beach Hotel, but her holiday was not remarkable for a burst of writing. A very different figure was impelled to write letters in his typically prophetic vein by Littlehampton's sea side. Again after a brief stop in Worthing, D. H. Lawrence in 1915, stayed at Bayford Road, one of the short streets of late nineteenth-century terraced houses leading from the boating pool to the High Street. The contrast between Coleridge playing with Fancy, inspired by the Classics, and the late Romantic poet and novelist in a mood of prophecy nearly a hundred years later is instructive.

D.H. Lawrence, almost in desperation, reaches out to the

sea as the last remnant of innocent and original nature: '. . . it is very healing, I think, to have all the land behind one, all this England with its weight of myriad amorphous houses, put back and only the variegated pebbles, and the little waves, and the great dividing line far off of sea and sky, with grey sailing ships like ghosts hovering motionless, suspended with thought. If only one could sweep clear this England of all its houses and pavements, so that we all could begin again' (Moore, H.T., ed., *Letters of D.H.Lawrence*, 1962, pp.357-358).

A few days later, Lawrence writes to Lady Asquith about the western shore of the Arun, even now a place apart from the town. From this vantage, the morphology of Litle hampton has changed, like the merging of the two parts of the name. The separation of 1817 - the town and harbour and the set-apart Beach Terrace - is over. To Lawrence the town is like any other - shapeless:

'Also over the river, beyond the ferry, there is the flat silvery world, as in the beginning, untouched with pale sand, and very much white foam, row after row, coming from under the sky in the silver evening, and no people, no people at all, no houses, no buildings, only a haystack on the edge of the shingle, and an old black mill. For the rest the flat unfinished world running with foam and noise and silvery light, and a few gulls, swinging like half born thoughts. It is a great thing to realise that the original world is still there - perfectly clean and pure, many white advancing foams, and only the gulls between the sky and the shore; and in the wind the yellow sea poppies fluttering very hard, like yellow gleams in the wind, and the windy flourish of the sea horns' (Moore - as above).

Lawrence turns to the town and finds it like 'a bad eruption on the edge of the land'. He feels sick of the ugliness seen from the clean West Beach, sick of the diseased spirit, 'Every landlady harping on her money, her furniture, every visitor harping on his latitude of escape from money and furniture'. Like Coleridge, he too saw a family by the beach. In 1915,

Lawrence noted a 'youth in a cap', his wife and a little child with whom they were playing on the beach. 'I think they were very poor'. To the angry writer, they appeared to be determinedly facing the sea away from the diseased land, trying to remain child-like.

Neither modern urban geographer nor Samuel Taylor Coleridge (even in his most haunted moments) would have pursued Lawrence's path of judgement. To the visitor from Highgate, it was not an 'amorphous' town. Little Hampton in 1817 had been a secure place, not a threat nor a symbol of what was wrong with the country. There were other places and other times for Coleridge to pursue that prophetic theme. In the small scale exclusion of Beach or South Terrace, he had found recovery. This was a moment not for rejection of the urban but a space where he could reshape his notes on the challenging immortality of the soul and reshape his health. They are fortunate places where one can so affirm. The town gave him a chance to write philosophy, to recover his health at least to an acceptable level - to endure. Then there was the wonderful luck of meeting two new friends. Of course, one must not forget - one good sonnet. Yes, a good holiday!

*The geography of towns is a branch of learning which thrives on play with metaphor. Because its subject is a complex of past and present with a dash of future hopes, urban geography must have intimate relations with other disciplines, such as history, sociology, and town planning. A discourse is required which can be shared, not a language private to the geographer. So, in the successive eras of urban studies, there have been many ways of explaining and describing what towns have been or are. In Robert Park's famous studies of Chicago and in the theories of Louis Wirth there was a strong dependence on biological and ecological analogy. Towns were like organisms. Then pattern making became the vogue, with 'morphology', the study of shapes and shaping, a way of defining what a town looked like from on top or horizontally as a townscape. Then with more (or, some said, less) mathematical modelling, construction of spatial models took on the task, combining planning and architectural modes, helping us to perceive successive changes. Reading the literature of the last fifty years of urban studies, one hears a refrain, a ground bass grumble that the people hidden in the description are never quite accounted for. The search for a human geography of towns assumes something like a mission - the quest for the people who lived in, felt about, and altered towns for reasons or for what they thought were reasons. Again, there is a temptation to pursue the quest by analogy with the living, not with organisms, but with human life. I shall succumb to that temptation chasing shape and time together in a brief encounter between a Sussex place and a person from Highgate, London.

SIXTEEN

Two Poems

Stephanie Norgate

GRIST
Iping December 1757

You play chess by the fire, your talk dozy
full of advent and farming. Outside
the little church squats
in the long window's view,
and the low barn roof
stretches down to the graves. Do you say,
'I'll come with you, Tom, a short way,'
and then, on a whim, walk on?
You can hear the mill,
turning ropes and rag and straw
into the pulp of paper. A blackbird
sings a warning near the parapet,
follows you both, along the cobbled path.
In sight of Stedham bridge, you stop.
The dark has come right in.
'I'll leave you now, Tom.' A handshake.
A shouted goodbye.

A damp walk back, a slight mist
curving over the river and rising
like a spirit, water translated.
You think, yes that's good,
or too pagan? You look again:
the mills, the iron, the hammer ponds,
the river of life, all grist for Sundays.
But why not rest, think only
this is just a river, this the rising mist?
That blackbird again. Your feet slip
in sandy mud.
'Good evening,' you cry,
thinking yes, this is good,
no analogy, just this,
the blackbird, the useful river
that drives the mills, that puts the food
in parish mouths, the farmhand
walking past you, the way
you want to touch him,
shake him by the hand, as you did
with Tom. And you stop, repeat
'Good evening. Richard Apps, is that you?'
You don't know why. But you have to ask
glimpsing suddenly the cold that's in him,
his legs bowed, his breath the stench of horses.
'Good evening. Tired, I suppose?'
You mean well, mean to tell
him that you know about the too early
mornings, the worms in his woman's
gut, that you forgive him for sending
back the ham. And you can't stop yourself,
'Come back with me and eat.'
You can't catch his words
only something of the way he'd once been forced
to eat a turd, to lay in dung, seen his father up
his mother, his sisters take their turn
in the one and only bed.

with which American singers travel. They dozed while the coach went round the M25, M23 and on down to Hove and there the parishioners were gathering like those adults we read about in children's story books set during war-time evacuation. Welcomes, introductions, dire-warnings about England's answer to poison-ivy, a rolls & coffee breakfast; and before we could match singers with host families already the questions began about the flint. They hadn't seen these shiny and irregular stones anywhere else, and they were captivated by the patterns on the napped face and the tradition of putting iron nails into the mortar to stop the devil creeping through the cracks.

The schedules on these trips (we did the first one in 1982) have slowly been simplified as the penny has dropped with the singers that there is more to be gained by an extended stay in a few places than leaping on and off the coach like a young hart and accumulating cathedrals and major churches in which they'd sung. I remember on one tour the American agents had arranged three Evensongs in Lincoln, but with a lunchtime recital in York on the second day of the three, and the way the trebles especially were wilting before He had 'put down the mighty from their seats' that day.

So having taken charge of these tours with others from Chichester Cathedral, we fixed a simple first weekend. On the Friday afternoon we met up for a drive around the area (although between the breakfast and the tour I'd had to make an unplanned trip to Heathrow to swap a bag due to have arrived in Beirut for one gentleman's own luggage he'd not actually seen). A bracing walk along the front at Brighton between the joggers and the families with ice cream and candy-floss worked up the appetite for dinner. The boys' conversations were already full of exchanged impressions about the English eccentricities and strange stereotyped expectations of Americans their hosts possessed. Saturday began with a rehearsal followed by a Civic Reception in the glossy modernity of Hove Town Hall and an exchange of gifts. The group were pleased by the welcome but in the evaluation they'd have preferred the chance to see something older in the time. That afternoon we made a trip over to Chichester.

On our first outing from Hove we had stopped on the way because some of the group had spotted Lancing College Chapel from the main road, so I guided John round past the *Sussex Pad* and he drove the coach over all those sleeping policemen up Lancing College drive. Remember that for most of the boys and for some of the adults this was their first big English church, and the length of the chapel and the brilliance of the rose window made them catch their breath.

'Say, can we just come in here like this?' asked one of the teenagers.

'Sure,' said another. 'Mr Gudderidge (they just can't cope with that double-t sound!) knows everyone.' As it happened, I was pushing the bounds of hospitality slightly in that my friend Ian Forrester, who was then the Chaplain at Lancing, and his family were in France, but on we all went, undaunted. The group clustered at the bottom of the chancel steps until their Director, Richard Webster, hummed some notes and the group broke into Bruckner's 'Locus iste', an unaccompanied motet they knew by heart. Lancing didn't offer the acoustic they found later in the Lady Chapel at Ely Chapel or the men's changing room at the municipal swimming pool in Coventry for the piece, but the vaulted space and the reflective surfaces of the principal Woodard chapel gave them plenty of scope for musical dynamics. Having looked and sung the choir poured out of the chapel and before I could load them up they were ambling round the terrace and looking out across the hillside, past the ponies grazing near the masters' houses, and down towards the airport at Shoreham. We loaded up and continued westwards. Looking up the Arun valley I had a chance to give a bit of an explanation of the flint industry and the chalk pits in the Downs.

Why they always shut it on Saturdays I don't know! We reached Arundel and of course they wanted to see the castle. Instead the children and a few adults followed me while the others explored by themselves. We went down to the lake and saw some of the castle from the walls, made the inevitable Rest Stop, and then climbed the High Street to the Catholic Cathedral, where we'd agreed to meet the rest of the party and John with the coach. In this county ecumenical relations between the Anglican and Roman Catholic communities are so much warmer than they are in Chicago. There the Episcopalians see the Romans as repressive and money-grabbing authoritarians, and the Romans regard the Anglicans as unprincipled liberals. So the choir was surprised by the fact that we went in two Roman churches that day and they'd be even more astonished to know that this year the Church of England's Bishop of Horsham held his confirmations for the Arundel & Bognor deanery in Arundel Cathedral.

We reached Chichester after a little diversion so that a military aviation enthusiast could see Tangmere Airfield. The first demand was to be allowed to go up the spire (not possible for visitors) but I promised a later visit to the Ringing Chamber of the Bell Tower. (You can do that. If you wait by the noticeboards at the top of the six broad steps leading to the glass doors at the West Front during bell practice on a Wednesday evening a ringer will come down to fetch you during a pause between pieces if you wave vigorously. You can climb the steps into the bottom of the Bell Tower where some of the bulky things from the cathedral are stored and then up inside until you come to the Ringing Chamber itself. The ropes and their sallies hand down in a circle and there are mats below for the ringers. It's worth the climb; the views are restricted by the cathedral, but there are some fascinating archive photos and prints, and it's not that noisy.) So, in. We established that even the youngest singer realized it was a church and that it was old. In Chicago almost only the stone water tower remained after an inferno raged through the city at the end of the last century, so everything is modern there: here sandstone from France transported across the channel in the eleventh century houses tapestry and glass from our own era. They stood almost transfixed by the colours of the Piper tapestry and the sounds of the organ.

Talk to them in terms they understand; so having marched directly to Bishop Eric's *cathedra* to see where the church gets its name, we then turned on our heels, back to the choir stalls themselves. The distance between trebles' stalls on decani and cantoris is the smallest of any Cathedral. Indeed, I can distribute papers to both sides simultaneously. As the visitors looked at the details in the carving of the pew-ends and the fronts of the desks I described a day in a Chichester chorister's working week. Wake up in a Prebendal School dormitory and have your feet hit the floorboards by 7:15 am. In Long Dorm, which runs the length of the original flint schoolhouse on West Street, there are old beams with plaques from the early nineteenth century bearing the names of Nelsons, and a spiral staircase in the south-west corner down to the basement three storeys below. By 7:30 you've to be in your practice room to do half-an-hour on the piano or your orchestral instrument before you line up for breakfast. Then Prayers, classes and an hour of choir practice - and all that before lunch!

These Chicago boys don't have a choir school. They come from the local Elementary and Junior High Schools to the Parish House to rehearse at the end of a working day, and perhaps to sing a weekly Evensong as well as a Sunday service. The discipline of daily rehearsal and daily Evensong on the tour pushes the musical standards they achieve ever higher, but now, at the beginning of the trip, the daily schedule causes eyebrows to rise and brows to furrow. I lead the way out under the Arundel Screen and over to the enormous door behind which a wide spiral stone staircase climbs up to the Chapter House and Song School. Of course, they want to go to the top!

As they come through the door and down into the room a smile of recognition creeps up the corners of their mouths.

TWENTY

Beginning at Arundel

Nick Warburton

Arundel, the early green of summer and the visitors have arrived.

They've come from the vast bleached grounds of Melbourne, Adelaide and Sydney where they will have hardened their game in front of the blunt opinions of the Hill, so they'll find little Arundel, with its deck-chairs, its polite, encouragement and its marquees erected in the lee of an ancient castle, rather strange. It seems an unlikely beginning to a tour, but perhaps the cricketing authorities know what they're doing. Perhaps sending the Australians into Sussex is more a sign of careful planning than English eccentricity. After all, the way the game is played depends on *where* it's played. So, don't start them at the great urban arenas of Edgbaston, Old Trafford or the Oval. Send them instead to Arundel. Tell them they are to play a pipe-opener against the Duchess of Norfolk's XI. That's right: the Duchess of Norfolk, whose home, of course, is in Sussex. Were you to follow logic and go to Norfolk in search of this fixture, you'd find the home of the Leicesters. You're in England now. It's all slightly different. And you will remember that this first game should not be taken too seriously, won't you? It's rather like village cricket, you see: no one will mind, or even remember, who wins.

Yes, begin at Arundel, and then move on to Worcester where cricketers have been know to swim across the square during the out-of-season flooding, and where you will be

JAHORE
An Indian prince at Jahore
Once knocked up at cricket a score
Which caused a sensation
Throughout the whole nation
For it beat all the records, and more.
VERSE BY G. E. FARROW; PICTURE BY JOHN HASSALL
Round the World ABC (Ernest Nister, 1904)

overshadowed by a cathedral.

The Arundel game is not the only aristrocratic aspect of Sussex cricket. The county's greatest players - Fry and Ranji - were both lorldly men, on and off the field. Charles Burgess Fry played football and cricket for his country. He held the world long-jump record for twenty-one years, was a distinguished classical scholar and was offered the throne of Albania. He declined the offer but would probably have made a striking king. He was a considerable writer, too. According to Neville Cardus, his book *Batsmanship* (1912) 'might conceivably have come from the pen of Aristotle had Aristotle lived nowadays and played cricket'.

Ranji - K. S. Ranjitsinhji, the Maharaja Jam Saheb of Nawanagar - kept a house in Sussex, Shillinglee Park, and both Fry and the elderly W. G. Grace would accept invitations to play there. There's a wonderful photograph of Ranji, taken in 1901. It shows him on the charge, dancing through the air, bat aloft, and it confirms him as a prince. Fry and Ranji are long gone, of course, but in 1961, when I saw cricket for the first time, Ted Dexter was playing for England. Dexter was another in the line of Sussex nobility! 'Lord' Ted they called him, and it was easy to see why. Wisden records that his 180 in the first Test Match of that year was 'a superb innings of stylish forceful strokes'.

I say that I first saw cricket in '61, but I really mean that I first understood it then. Before that summer I'd been bored by the very idea of the thing. I'd walked past radios and heard John Arlott or Rex Alston talking about it - endlessly and pointlessly it seemed - and I was familiar with a handful of famous names: Dexter, of course, Cowdrey and May and Freddie Trueman. It was impossible not to know *something* about cricket in those days. But it was just a game to me: there was nothing else to say about it.

This first proper encounter was also in Sussex. Not at Arundel, but Eastbourne. And not at the Saffrons, but on a little black and white television set in my uncle's guest house.

It's early June and sunny. Eastbourne is as foreign to me as Arundel probably appears to visiting tourists. In 1961 it's nothing like my home on the fringes of the East End. As far as I can tell, Eastbourne has no hard-brick council estates. There are no youths lounging against school railings and staring hard at you as you pass.
'You looking at my hat?'
'No.'
'Why? What's wrong with it?'
No, youths in Eastbourne are deferential and wear blazers. The streets are broad and lined with full-sized trees. Somewhere on the other side of town there is the sea and rich grass slopes that sweep up to Beachy Head. Even Eastbourne sandwiches are different, cut in neat triangles rather than half squares. My uncle's place is different too. It's so big you can climb one staircase, wander about upstairs on long red carpets, and come down a different set of stairs to find yourself in some other, unfamiliar and slightly threatening part of the house.

We are in the garden and can see the television with its doors open relaying the Test Match to an empty room. A fascinating room, though. Big armchairs, a wind-up gramophone, sheet music hidden in a piano stool. Outside with the others, I charge up and down the lawn, scrabbling for tennis balls in the bushes. Then wander in to catch my breath and glance at the set. On it, Australia batting. Someone calls from the garden.
'Mackay still in?'
I don't know, I've never heard of Mackay, but a man is pacing up and down by some stumps, frowning with concentration, chewing.

'Still in,' I call back, hoping I'm right. I am. The Australian all-rounder Ken Mackay is a dour batsman, well aware that he has five full days to make his mark on the game. Slasher Mackay, they call him, but the name, is ironic. I watch for some time and never see him slash at the ball. He prods. And England can't get rid of him. He makes 64 in, as Wisden puts it, 'his own characteristic way'.

More illustrious Australians than Mackay were involved in that Eastbourne Test Match. (It was played at Edgbaston not Eastbourne, but I still think of it as the Eastbourne Test.) Neil Harvey scored a hundred and Richie Benaud captained the side, but it was in the dogged, unlikely Mackay that I first saw something of the true nature of cricket. I went home, a lover of the game, to watch my own county, Essex, play, at Leyton.

Leyton is a London ground, not at all like Saffrons, but just as lovely in its idiosyncratic, grimy way, and the cricket played there owes something to the spirit of the place. Eastbourne or Arundel would not have done for South West Essex: too leafy and not enough brick. If you play in London you must carve pitches out of recreation grounds and bat beneath gas-works and behind concrete fencing, with dog muck in the grey-green outfield and graffiti all over the changing rooms. It's good cricket too, but not the cricket they play in Sussex, in downland villages and by the sea.

A wet Saturday in Chichester. Late Sixties. Warm, heavy rain all morning so we all assume the game between the college and a local village will be called off.
'No,' they say. 'You come along. Our ground dries very quickly.'

It does, but the pitch cooks under the afternoon sun and becomes sticky. You can stamp on it and almost see the ripples. The grass is lush and cows are still grazing on it when the stumps are set, so the village send their twelfth man out to chase them off with a pair of pads. They have a traditional fearsome-looking blacksmith playing for them. A tall man, black-haired, with side whiskers like hatchets. We eye him and mutter to each other, dreading the moment when he comes on to bowl. He's uncharacteristic of the blacksmiths of legend, though, and loops the ball gently through the air, only occasionally making it pitch. But the ball loves that cow-pat surface when I bowl. It jags and turns - I can see it doing so, thirty years later. A friend, persuaded to play with false promises that he won't be called upon to bat or bowl, hides under some overhanging trees at long off. It's somehow inevitable that a catch will come his way. It drills through his frightened fingers and leaves a perfect imprint of the seam on his bruised chest. We stand over him, cursing his ineptitude. This is Sussex village cricket.

Another Saturday, later in the season. We find ourselves playing no more than a lofted drive from the sea. At Selsey, perhaps. Large ships move slowly behind the bowler's arm and everyone must sit down until they've passed. Mid-way through the afternoon, a sea fret eases across the field and suddenly the man with the ball discovers he can bend it through the mist. He takes six wickets. Effortlessly. But he's a rugby man at heart and just happened to be in the right place at the right time. It's his first and last bowl of the season.

The nearest we get to the spirit of Arundel is Priory Park in Chichester. We're too young and inexperienced to make any impact on the Town XI, but we're pleased to be playing on a ground so quintessentially Sussex. Where Grace himself once played, we're told. That same Grace who batted along-side Fry and Ranji, the Sussex aristocracy, and put the visiting Australians to the sword.

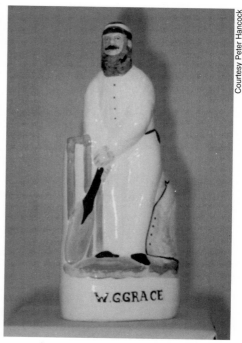

Courtesy Peter Hancock

W. G. GRACE
*recent model of the popular
Staffordshire figure*

TWENTY-ONE

'And the Sperrit of her is with the Bürrd'

Maggie Roberts

'Cup of tea?'

I nod my reply, smiling at these three words - Cup of tea, a nice cup of tea.

I like a nice cup of tea in the morning, I like a nice cup of tea with my tea and round about eleven my idea of heaven is a nice… cup of tea to lift your spirits; calm you down; buffer against bad tidings. My mother and I surmise that her epitaph could well be 'A nice cup of tea' and she laughs at the thought - we are not squeamish about THE END: it is as inevitable as the seasons and the sunrise. We accept its place in the cycle of Life, even if its timing seems seldom right for any of us.

We talk about the family; the state of the world (to which we have ALL the answers, if only we were in charge); the village and all its changes. We are in the living room and as I look out across the stretch of green that marks the boundary of my parents' home, my mother informs me that MORE houses are to be built in the village. What is worse, they are to be constructed just yards from where we are sitting. The rooks will lose their homes whilst those who can afford the four and five bedroomed 'prestigious' dwellings will be cheek by jowl with (ex) council houses - 'Not that they look like it, of course', my mother adds carefully.

In 1967, when the Roberts family (including goldfish) moved to Tangmere, I didn't even know what a 'village' was. At the grand age of eight years and nine months I knew only of the city (Plymouth) and the country (Dartmoor) - nothing existed outside these two extremes. In those days, Tangmere was two villages - The RAF village and the 'real' village. Nearly all the children I met up with on my walk to school were from 'the camp'. The dividing line between us was geographical rather than social, with the RAF houses being at the 'top' of the village, between the Guardhouse and the busy A27, and the village 'proper' running from the tiny local store, beside the sweeping willows on the corner of Chestnut Walk, to the airfield alongside the Tangmere 'straight'. Despite the division, the children from the two villages played as one.

The old cattle-pens on the farm near the Church were favourite haunts to many. The farmland was bounded by deep (or so they seemed to us) drainage ditches, and it was in these damp trenches that myself, and my best friend Carol, would hunt for flowers to give to our mothers on Mothering Sunday. Violet bluebells, pale lemon primroses, campions the colour of powdered-rouge and best of all, Lent-lilies. These lightly perfumed, wild daffodils grew in scattered clumps, in the field adjacent to the old rectory. Their delicately-scented petals ranged from palest cream to chaffinch yellow and buttercup gold. They hinted at mellow summer evenings and the warmth to come.

'The air was keen and still as I walked back in the early evenings and a daffodil light was in the sky as if Heaven mirrored back earth's radiance.
Near the station some children-flitted past, like little white miller moths homing through the dusk. As I climbed the hill the moon rode high in the golden field - it was daffodils to the last.'

Tangmere is flat, very flat and its recorded history reaches back to the time of the Domesday Book, where it is referred to as Tang(e) mere. Some sources have suggested that there was a forked river in the locale, from which the name was derived;

the Norse word 'tang' meaning tongs. However, evidence from soil surveys cast doubt on this theory, as the minute deposits of shell fragments found in the ground are of the type that only exist in marshy environments. It would appear, then, that the place was probably made up of several shallow pools that came and went as the seasons changed but for the larger part it consisted of baggy reed-beds. Certainly, as a child I recall there was a pond by the outer wall of St Andrew's church. In those days it was a grassy hollow that mysteriously filled with water every spring and afforded a solitary pair of ducks a home. Now it is hemmed in with bricks and metal; a corral erected by developers who chose to call the cattle-pens they converted into bijou residences for the gentile elderly - 'Saxon Meadow'.

The church was another play area for the children of the two villages, although they chose to play around it rather than in or through it. For me the place held no fear. Rather it was a refuge from the demands of human interaction and the general din of life. I used to settle myself inside the hollow trunk of the ancient Yew and imagine that I had become one with its scaly bark and dark green spikes. In this manner I could become still and in this place of silence, survey the wild world, as if I too were one of its creatures.

Maggie Roberts

It was from this vantage point, one balmy evening, that I had a revelation. Above the lintel of a small window in the side of the church there is a carving of two figures and of this I was fully aware. However, until the evening sun lit up these forms in a way that seemed to animate them, it was as if I had never noticed them until that moment of re-seeing.

Crudely hewn, they contain an energy that naïve art achieves. Like a stone cartoon they tell a story, although what that tale meant to our pagan ancestors we can only guess at. The interpretation favoured by the church and reproduced in several articles about the lintel, is that one figure represents Salome who is holding out the severed head of John the Baptist to her mother. What I saw that evening and have seen ever since, is a ritual offering. One figure, the symbol of the sun-disc by its head, stretches out its hands to another figure with a sickle moon (waxing not waning) by its temple. In the hands of the sun-figure is a large horn tipped towards the bowl that the moon-figure extends.

A libation is being poured out at the time of fertility and plenty. Humankind and the natural world are fused in their need for food and warmth. The sun and moon control our destinies; science is magic and natural laws must be reinforced with human effort and energy. Christianity released us from the burden of helping the sun rise each day, but imposed its own penalties on the human spirit.

> *'We have banished the protecting gods that ruled in river and mountain, tree and grove; we gainsayed for the most part folk-lore and myth, superstition and fairytale, evil only in their abuse. We have done away with mystery or named it deceit.... There is more truth in the believing cry, 'Come from thy white cliffs, O Pan!' than in religion that measures a man's life by the letter of the Ten Commandments, and erects itself as judge and ruler over him instead of throwing open the gate of the garden where God walks with man from morning until morning.'*

I make to leave my mother after the tea, cakes and conversation are exhausted. She wonders if I might be interested in another of her book 'finds'. 'I'm only going to put it back in another jumble sale', she adds (the cycle of Life continues). She knows I will not refuse her offer - books are crammed full of secrets to be deciphered (as a child under the bedclothes by torchlight) and I love each literary journey, each reality waiting to be brought to life.

The slender tome has faded to the colour of a fox skirting the fields at dusk. The cloth cover is worn smooth and the pages smell of old drawing-rooms. Turning back the cream-edged pages I read the dedication:

TO MY MOTHER: AND TO EARTH, MY MOTHER,
WHOM I LOVE

Entitled *The Roadmender*, I see the compact book is written by a Michael Fairless, (1869-1901). The preface informs me that this publication has little need of introduction as it is 'universally known and loved'. I reflect that my education must be lacking, and read on.

Michael is not what he appears. George Sand and Ellis Bell amongst others bear witness to this fact. Michael was born Margaret Fairless Barber, the youngest of three daughters, to the lawyer, Fairless Barber and his wife Maria (Musgrave). A Yorkshire lass from Castle Hill, Rastrick, Michael moved to London to train as a nurse. In her youth, she worked in one of the worst slums in the East End of London, the Jago. Tall and quick-witted, she was a strong-spirited woman and became known as the Fighting Sister, for the manner in which she stood up for her patients - once knocking down a man who had forced his way into his sick wife's room!

However, her nursing career was cut short by a 'spinal weakness', legacy from her childhood. She ended up living in the lodge of an old abandoned manor house on the 'great Bath road', a semi-invalid, with 'a decrepit old woman and a mentally deficient girl' to care for her. At around this time she first came to be known by the Dowson family who adopted her into their own; Michael having neither parents to return to nor siblings who were able to care for her.

Michael had struggled with her desire to be creative, throughout her short life. Having been brought up to believe that artistic expression was of secondary importance in relation to service to others. Paradoxically, it was her own ill health that released her from this false belief. Unable to care for others as she had in the past and being forced to rest, she was at last given the permission she needed to freely explore and express her inner world.

The Roadmender was written during the last two years before her death in a farmhouse at Mock Bridge, Shermanbury, on the outskirts of Henfield. It is referred to as a 'devotional' work and the tale is allegorical in style. The central character, the roadmender, is not only Michael Fairless but is meant to represent all humankind;

THE YOUNG MICHAEL FAIRLESS
*- drawn by Elinor Dowson (c. 1912)
from a photograph*

as did Everyman in Bunyan's *Pilgrim's Progress*. Thus, the roadmender observes and records Life as it passes by, as well as participating in the lives of those he meets on their journeys; occasionally travelling with them. He also notes the changes occurring in the countryside at that time in history, as the mechanical reaper replaced the skilled farm labourer with his 'sibilant' scythe.

Throughout the book, although the philosophy is meant to be Christian, Michael's overwhelming love of the natural world seems more akin to the pagan:

'We can never be too Pagan when we are truly Christian, and the old myths are eternal truths held fast in the Church's net . . . . Earth my mother . . . I can never remember the time when I did not love her, this mother of mine with her wonderful garments and ordered loveliness, her tender care and patient bearing of man's burden.'

In the twenty months it took her to complete the book, Michael spent two summers in her beloved 'lean grey Downs'. The rest of the time she spent in an old Georgian house on the Chelsea Embankment, near the Thames. *The Roadmender*, too, moves from country to town and town to country. Michael's passion for the Sussex countryside and wildlife is reflected in the book and the simple wooden cross that marks her grave in Ashurst cemetery, says powerfully:

'Lo! How I loved thee.'

It is two weeks since I took charge of *The Roadmender* and I am about a third of the way through it. Michael's descriptions of spring serve to highlight the gloom I witness from my bedroom window. It is another grey and cloudy day. I feel as if someone has shut the world up in a shoe box and sealed the lid down. Winter seems never ending this year, especially after the dull excuse for last summer, that El Niño and El Niño ensured. Longing for the spring, I believe I understand why our ancestors kept the gods sweet with sacrifices - just to see the sun, some light, some life.

> *'My little tree is gemmed with buds, shy, immature, but full of promise. The sparrows busied with nest-building in the neighbouring pipes and gutters use it for a vantage ground, and crowd there in numbers, each little beak sealed with long golden straw or downy-feather . . . We stand for a moment at the meeting of the ways, the handclasp of Winter and Spring, of Sleep and Waking, of Life and Death . . .'*

My partner's mother dies suddenly and unexpectedly; three days later we watch a butterfly emerge from a crevice on the patio steps and proceed to warm itself, for a full quarter of an hour, in our first glimpse of February sunlight. Later that same day, a small finch the colour of pondweed, alights on the handle of the French windows and taps furiously at the glass, as if such action would afford it entry. At the back of my mind, recollections of such a tap, tap, tapping at a window pane at night. A young girl seeking a way back to earth. A pale hand ground down on broken glass; blood, pain and fear.

Cups of tea cannot comfort my partner. Tea and sympathy will not suffice and the attempts of others to console serve only to cause more pain. Before the wound scabs over, another kind word tears it off - the metaphor is clichéd but the emotions are unique. Death like Love is doomed to express itself in well-worn phrases, lacking in imagination. Words are not enough and my partner and I weep . . . apart; each fearing the other's neediness.

Mother's Day looms. Everywhere reminders of the loss. 'Special Four Course Meal for Mother's Day'; 'Oil of Ulay for Mother'; 'Send flowers to Mum - special delivery'. I venture a wry smile at this last - they'd have to be very 'special delivery', and then I feel guilt at the thought of such a thought. I try to distract my partner from seeing these messages - a ridiculous task, akin to Canute's. I make preparations for my own mother, secretly and as discreetly as I can.

Mothering Sunday arrives. A drive in the country has been planned. A day trip to visit Buncton, which sounds like Duncton with a heavy cold. We are aiming for the old church on the hill, which according to my father has an odd carving of a human form that he believes might interest me. He wonders if the figure could be pagan, akin to the couple on the lintel at Tangmere Church. Curiosity awakened, I am six years old again and make sure I am first out of the car and up the twisting, muddy pathway to the summit, before all others.

The sky matches the bluebells we encounter en route. The sun is high and hot. As we mount the brow of the hill, we are afforded the first glimpse of the church, which seems to grow out of the earth itself, like a large granary loaf. On closer inspection I see why it gives this impression - the walls are an eclectic collection of bricks, flint and stone; some of which, according to the literature inside the building, date back to Roman times. My father points out the 'pagan' carving. The figure disappoints. It is thin and pale and its nether regions have been scythed away so that gender is indecipherable. I peer closer: it has a sad face and tiny, tight breasts, but somehow it doesn't look female. I decide it is probably Saxon but it is not pagan, no pagan would depict a god or goddess so. There is fear in this figure and frailty - I am reminded of Adam in the garden, suddenly aware that he is unclothed. This is no god, this figure is human; naked, afraid and alone. I left *The Roadmender* in England, two and a half hours flight away. I reflect that I should have left the dismal weather there too. Today the clouds have bubbled-up from the turquoise sea and the sky above Sousse is chalky white - a Sussex sky. From the balcony, I see it is raining; a gentle, soft rain that moistens the sandy soil from beige to pale orange. Traffic hisses on the glistening tarmac. Everything is damp and warm. My partner too, is damp with sweat, and hot and cold by turns. A sore throat has turned to bronchitis for the second time this year. The body expressing what the mind struggles to acknowledge. Memories surface in this place we had hoped to escape them - the loss of the mother is rekindled in sickness.

I wash the bitter scent of perspiration from my partner's clothes and drape the garments over the white-washed balcony, to dry in the evening sun. In the swaying trees, birds chatter and call to each other - sparrows, blackbirds and starlings; their evensongs I am familiar with in this unfamiliar place. On the ledge of the balcony, I have scattered bread for the birds and half-filled an ashtray with water. My partner wakes to witness a pale green finch dive down and carry off a crumb of bread. In our exchanged glances we share the same thought. But these are (post) modern times; God is dead and the human soul a mere product of imagination; the spirit, reduced to a genetic bar-code. 'She loved the birds' - my partner longs for faith; to believe, just for a while, that something persists beyond the corporeal. It is the blankness of death that confuses us. We seek signs, for reassurance.

'A follerin' bürrd,' he said.

I got up, and looked across the blue field we were ploughing into white furrows. Far away a tiny sail scarred the great solitude, and astern came a gull flying slowly close to the water's breast.

Daddy Whiddon waved his pipe towards it.

'A follerin' bürrd,' he said, again . . . .

' . . . and the sperrit of her is with the bürrd'.

TWENTY-TWO

SPLITTING THE SEAM

Wendy Scott

Splitting the seam or splitting the screen?
And does it amount to the same?
Was it a blur of a postmodern world,
Or a picture in search of a frame?

The old are too old to remember the past,
And the young are too young to care.
But those of us neither too young nor too old
Were never afraid to dare.

For that is the lure, and that is the thrill,
And that is the challenge to win.
You will, if you will
And you will . . . and you will . . .
And glamour is never a sin.

Spare a thought briefly, if briefly you might,
For the journey that crossed the seam.
The toiling up to the top of the ridge,
And the flowing down with the stream.

After the splitting the healing begins
And now we are coasting the downs.
A trio of swallows swoops over the fields -
A patchwork of greens and browns.

The selvage is bound to the edge of the seam
With stitches that melt in the fold.
The downlands are patterned with bracken and furze
In a tapestry woven with gold.

TWENTY-THREE

RIDING THE SOUTH DOWNS

Andrew Flaherty

I am one of the unwashed, the unloved, the outcasts. Why? You may ask! It is partly for my love of clothing, tight and shiny, but also for the fact that my preferred means of getting around the hills and valleys has two wheels and no legs. As you may guess, my mountain bike and I go everywhere.

Many rights of way acknowledge that there are members of the public like myself who don't always like to walk. The alternative, riding a horse, is probably even more alarming, due to the fact that they don't have brakes, as well as the fact that they have a brain of their own - one of those traumatic childhood experiences, I'm afraid.

Fortunately the South Downs has, like many other upland areas, an ancient right of way for horses and animals which now include riders on our metal steeds. Living and working around Chichester gives me access to some of the most beautiful and dramatic landscape to be found in Southern Britain. Further, my good fortune to have lived in two different parts of Sussex has given me a great appreciation of the changing looks of the Downs and of our affect upon them.

Before moving to Chichester I lived in Hove, with its long sweeping climbs rising from the sea past places such as Skeleton Hovel, strangely now a Golf Club, Scabes Castle and Mount Zion, before finally topping out upon the Devil's Dyke. This last is a strangely desolate place with the northern scarp face dropping away from the viewer and providing huge vistas up towards Hurstpierpoint and Henfield; but, at the same time, offering a feeling that one could have come here a millennia ago and the scene would have been similar - except, perhaps, for the pub, which for me is a perfect example of how not to take a place that is almost mystical and transform it utterly into something commercial, devoid of the resonances of history.

From this point high on the Downs, one can turn west and head off downhill towards Truleigh Hill and the radio masts. It is ironic how so many of the results of our modern lives impinge on us just at those times when we are trying to escape them. My last trip along this stretch of downland led to an encounter with my arch nemesis, Ramblers. These marauding groups of people, often forty to fifty strong, amble purposefully (I grant) from place to place; but although we get along amicably when encountered singly or in pairs, in a group they can become militant. Passing a group of this size entails going at a snail's pace, as they refuse to yield, and to being subjected to calls of 'Get off that bike and walk!' or 'Slow down!' How being on foot infuses one with a moral superiority has always puzzled me; horse-riders never behave like this.

The next stretch of this downland ride is the drop down from Truleigh, which leads into one of my favourite sections, the climb up to Chanctonbury Ring from the River Adur. This slightly masochistic trait, of delighting in the *uphill*, bemuses my partner who much prefers going *down* to *up* but for me, that lung-bursting pressure as one reaches the top is so much more rewarding - it celebrates one's physicality and affirms that one is alive. Chanctonbury Ring itself is an eerie and spiritual area, especially on a cold February morning when the frost on the trees gives a hint of Narnia about everything, or towards twilight as the boundaries between us and them begin to thin.

Chanctonbury and the drop onto the A24 unfortunately mean the end of interesting countryside for a while, as the section from here to Amberley is desolate and dull. Such a view is probably flavoured by the fact that, usually, one is cycling against the prevailing wind and, also, it always seems to be raining! There is, however, some compensation for it seems that whenever I am there, there is also a man with a Labrador: where he comes from or goes to I am not sure as, being English, we always stop to speak but only talk about the weather.

From Amberley there is the long climb up past Houghton onto the high ground and then up to Bignor Hill. From here westwards, the character of the land changes completely as we move from a very open and stark landscape to one that is strewn with

IN THE MIND'S EYE; OR, HOW A CYCLIST SEES A JOURNEY (IN RETROSPECT)

- note the omission of distances and compass points, but the incorporation of viewpoints, the use of idiosyncratic orthography, and the way the bicycle pictograph seems not to indicate gradients

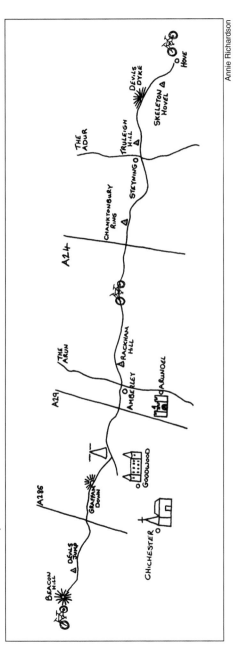

Annie Richardson

woodland old and new. The hill lines also change - from having only one main set to having two: one splits off towards Goodwood and the coastal defences above Portsmouth, and the other leads further north and west, to finish in Winchester. It is the land between these two hill-lines has been my playground since I moved to Chichester, but the Downs still form the backbone of what I enjoy.

From Bignor Hill one passes another sign of man's intrusion, the masts just before Sutton Down, and then a nice easy decent to the A285. After that, my partner and I have a knee-straining climb back up to Littleton Down where there is always the decision of whether to carry on or head down towards East Dean and Goodwood. The riding between here and the drop down to the road south of Cocking is where some of the most fun on the Downs to be had, as it is relatively flat with plenty of cover for both summer and winter. The final run down to the road is a loose chalk track showing the effect of both man, through vehicles, and nature, through rain, in trying to turn a flat surface into a river bed.

Emerging from the car park on the main road the nicest users of the South Downs can be found; the dog walkers. I do not know what it is but the presence of a dog seems to turn the most hardened rambler into a chatty friendly human being. Following in their footsteps we head up the hill towards Cocking Down, past the oddly named Linch Ball, and finally take a detour off the most direct route past the Devils Jumps. Why some jumps are humps and some humps are jumps is still a puzzle to me and probably lost in the mists of time.

The final climb of the journey is the one up to Beacon Hill. Even in the middle of summer this hill seems to be too far for most people to walk so it has a wonderfully peaceful feel about it, although erosion bears testimony to the number of people who still make the pilgrimage. This peacefulness means that Beacon Hill has a special feel for me - possibly because of the views or, possibly, because it is the end of my journey before heading home.

Man is evident in all aspects of the South Downs Way, with many groups claiming to have priority over other users, whether they are on foot, on horseback or riding a cycle or, indeed, whether they live and work on the downs themselves. Nevertheless, the damage of our presence, whoever we are, is plain for all to see so I think we must all try to step a little lighter so that we all have something to pass on to our children - for them to argue over, and to treasure.

Without man's intrusion into the countryside, we would not have the South Downs Way: it is striking the balance of use that will always be difficult.

The Ring and the Haven
(THREE POEMS FOR SHAUN)

Rilla Dudley

CAMERA AT CUCKMERE HAVEN

I wait for stillness.

Paper-thin petals waver at a wind's whisper;
spring-boarding grasshoppers enliven the sward;
stamens succumb to a bee's business,
and exhausting too many notes,
a lark falls to earth.

The tide retreats from white cliffs.
The pebble shore expands.
The sea is a heaving stage,
bright-lit or darkened, as the sun slips
between shifting clouds.

Butterflies pause momentarily,
wings sun-spread; then shut at a shadow.
Rising with a breeze,
fast, erratic, they dance away.

I wait for stillness.

CUCKMERE HAVEN FROM CISSBURY RING

Rising from the dark sea to a dusk-washed sky,
one chalk cliff is sunstruck gold.
Here, like confetti, your ashes
will scatter over Downland,
like Blues, settle on scabious,
or dancing away, drift out to sea.
Already, standing in cloud shadows
on the rain weeping hill,
your spirit is the caught light
in the distant view.

CISSBURY RING

She sees a face as white as blossom,
a body still as a felled tree;
only the eyes, dark as earth,
are speaking; she shares their dreams.

She sees pictures of wild roses,
thyme cushions, quaking grass;
sees him in butterfly clouds,
standing higher than swallows,
surveying sheep-filled Downs;
sees him fading like the worn painted ladies,
dulled brown on dry earth;
sees him lying on the green sward,
fading, fading, into the white chalk.

In Downs' time
all their footsteps
not even a sigh.

TWENTY-FIVE

Christopher Aggs: The Coast Road - View from Mill Hill, Shoreham (November 1998)

From this point, in the car park on Mill Hill, one could turn slightly to the west to draw the famously picturesque view of Lancing College Chapel that dominates the gap in the downs cut by the River Adur. Instead, in this drawing and an accompanying series of paintings, the choice was made to look at the way transport influences our view of the landscape. The A27 crosses the river just upstream of the old footbridge, and beyond these bridges Shoreham Airport stretches towards the sea, with the coastal railway line lying in between. In the centre are the flattened ellipses of the 'clover leaf' junction - which are very attractive to an artist.

Civil engineers and road planners, so often vilified, can be.seen as the unrecognized sculptors of the late twentieth century. The rather misty late afternoon light somewhat romanticises the scene, but it also brings a sense of history to the view. Edward Burra, in his sequence of downland watercolours of the 1960s, treated railways and trunk roads as intruders on the landscape, although one also senses a sneaking admiration for the grandeur of the engineering - see, for example, those featured in Andrew Causey, *Edward Burra: Complete Catalogue* (Phaidon, Oxford; 1985)

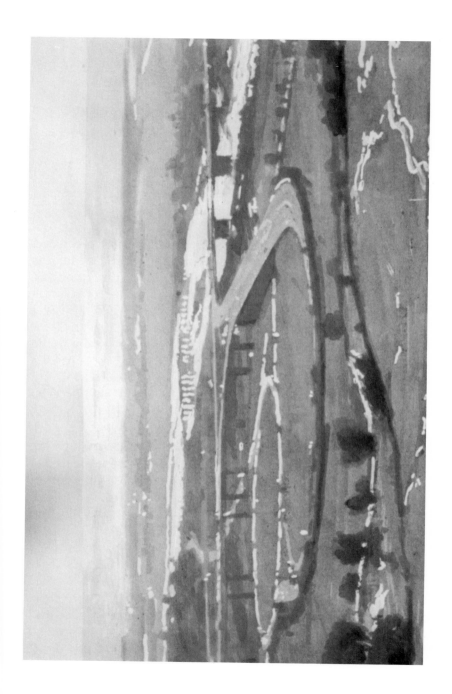

'A Choice of Strawberries or Peaches': Exploring Sussex with S.P.B. Mais

Timothy J. McCann

On 17 July 1997, West Sussex County Council erected a plaque in Southwick in honour of Stuart Petre Brodie Mais, as part of their programme, initiated in 1992, of commemorating distinguished people of Sussex. The plaque was erected at the Hall in Southwick, and reads 'S.P.B. Mais 1885-1975, novelist travel writer Champion of Cricket lived here 1927-1932'. 1 have discussed Mais as a champion of cricket elsewhere in the pages of the *Journal of the Cricket Society*, and I am not in a position to discuss his merits as a novelist, but I would like to say something about his career as a travel writer. The following account discusses his travel writings in general, and, in particular, his writings on and about Sussex.

Mais was born in Cornwall and brought up at Tansley near Matlock, where his father was incumbent. He was educated at Denstone and Christ Church Oxford, where he was an athletics blue and went down with a poor degree. For a time he taught at Rossall, Sherborne and then at Tonbridge before becoming the first Professor of English at RAF Cranwell. After his unorthodox teaching career was brought to a premature end by what he described in *A Schoolmaster's Diary* as his encouragement of free expression and his passion for educational reform, he became a journalist. On the *Daily Express* and the *Daily Graphic* he acted as literary critic and dramatic critic as well as gossip columnist before becoming a leader-writer on the *Daily Telegraph*. In 1930, at the age of 45, he was made redundant, and for the rest of his life he practised as a freelance journalist, broadcaster and writer. He is still remembered by many people for his broadcasting and is said to have written more than 170 books.

His first success as an author was achieved by writing standard English textbooks. *An English Course for Schools* in 1919 and *An English Course for Everybody* in 1921, were bestsellers, but did not provide sufficient income on their own to compensate for the loss of his salary as a journalist. Several of his novels are set in Sussex - *Caged Birds* (1922) and *Quest Sinister* (1922) in Brighton district, some of *Eclipse* (1925) is set in the Angmering area; as is *Orange Street* (1926)); while *First Quarter* (1929) is set in Southwick itself; the action of *Frolic Lady* (1930) takes place on the Sussex coast and Downland between Brighton and Goring - but their popularity does not seem to have lasted, and they were not particularly profitable. Rather it is his many travel books that are worth looking out for, and especially the series of family travel books he wrote for Christopher Johnson after the Second World War, and which he launched with *I return to Scotland* in 1947.

Mais's travel writing can be divided into three types and each type was characterised by a different style. His pre-war travel books, mostly devoted to the British Isles, are written in a full-bodied style. They positively bounce with personality, enthusiasm and drive. His post-war travel books, mostly devoted to Europe and further afield, are quite different. In a sense they reflect the austerity of the post-war tourist gradually re-discovering the European experience. They are composed of short pithy sentences, packed

Mais Family archive

MAIS INTRODUCES THE DELIGHTS
OF THE COUNTRYSIDE TO HIS
DAUGHTER LALAGE
1938

with information, and detail the life of an ordinary family on holiday.* Finally his travel writings devoted to Sussex, and Southwick in particular, are characterised by the unrestrained Mais treatment: lyrical descriptions, passionate responses to atmosphere and place, and a great love of the locality where he made his emotional and physical home.

In his early travel books, Mais made a point of playing the xenophobic Englishman, and his preface to *See England First* (1937) is a typical example.

'I have long believed that there is a conspiracy of silence on the part of all returned travellers,' he wrote: 'they all come back disappointed, but they dare not confess that their time was wasted, their money ill-spent . . . What I would know is this: when the woods in April are star-whitened with anemones or outrival the azured air with the blueness of their bluebells, when hedges are yellow with cowslips and primroses and the banks of trout-streams are lit up with the golden splendour of marsh-marigolds, has the world anything to show more fair?' And he went on to contrast the wonders of the unknown with the scant justice afforded to the familiar, comparing the Acropolis and the Parthenon unfavourably with Haddon Hall or Salisbury Cathedral.

'When the travellers come back from Samarkand and Cathay,' he continued, 'they have nothing to tell me which makes me feel that I have missed anything for which I would miss an English spring. What have they to tell that compares with the sight of lilac and laburnam, of woods carpeted with anemones and bluebells, of days spent partly browning on the beach and partly diving into deep water, of games of tennis under a blue sky, of bowling at the nets, of sailing up and down the creeks at Bosham, of footpaths when the moon is up and all the air is still, of lazing on green lawns, or dozing in hammocks soothed by the hum of bees and the pleasant warm scent of mignonette and wall-flowers?'

*See p.182

There was always a chapter about Sussex in his early travel books, such as *Oh! To be in England* (1922), *See England First* (1927), *It Isn't Far from London* (1930), which includes a chapter on Goodwood and an effusive description of walking on the South Downs, and *Round about England* (1935). Indeed four of the thirteen chapters in *See England First* are devoted to the county, and he further expounded his philosophy of travel in the book by declaring two important rules - 'the first is to sell your car and the second is never to lunch at home'. 'No', he wrote, 'the only way is to walk and to be out all day.' He firmly believed that the English midday meal more than anything else, stood in the way of our discovering our own country. He advocated starting from a suitable centre, usually wherever he happened to live at the time - and he preferred to travel to the start of his walk by bus rather than by train. 'In a train one's fellow-travellers are citizens of the world and one misses the scenery', he said, 'but on a bus you get into touch with the Sussex people, and you have time to appreciate the changing scenery.'

He had to change his advice when he was asked to write his three booklets for the Southern Railway. 'I have just boarded any train and got out of it when the countryside looked inviting,' he explained in *Southern Rambles*. 'It is a magnificent proof of England's loveliness that I have never failed to find beauty. I like generally to walk from north to south, or from east to west in order to have the sun in my face, but I also like to have the wind at my back, and that has caused me often to disregard my sun-rule. I like to have as short a train journey as possible to begin with, for I am always fretful until I take to my legs. In the evening, when I am deliciously tired, I like a longer time in the train to ruminate upon the adventures that I have encountered and to conjure up afresh visions of the beauty that has been vouchsafed to me during the day.' He was commissioned to write several booklets on the county, such as *The Official Handbook to the Corporation of Brighton* (1930) or *Around Brighton: Footpath Guide no.40* (1948) or *The Land of the Cinque Ports* in 1949, for after all he was a professional writer, but he wrote only one book completely dedicated to his adopted county.

In 1929 Mais published a small book entitled simply *Sussex*. It begins with a characteristic dedication:

> To those school-children and members of the hockey and cricket elevens who play upon the Green, and to all those other inhabitants of and visitors to the village of Southwick who have contributed so overwhelmingly to my happiness I dedicate, with affection and gratitude, this book.

He introduces the book by stating that he makes no excuse whatever for adding one more to the hundreds of books on Sussex. 'Better writers than I can ever hope to be have written about it, better men than I can ever hope to be have loved it better than I have, but I dare swear that no man has found so much happiness in it as I have, and happiness has been none too easy to find in our post-war world. Sussex is not the county of my birth, but it is the county of my adoption. I was not privileged to be born in it, but I hope that nothing will prevent me from living in it until I die. In my eyes it has but one drawback. It ruins one for everywhere else.'

On exploring Sussex he says, 'The best way, in my opinion,' he concludes, 'is the way of the child faced with a choice of strawberries or

Mais Family archive

MAIS OUT WALKING
(date unknown)

178

peaches - a little, meaning as much as possible, of both. To explore Sussex properly one ought to adopt the practice once in vogue among our more voluble paper-saving aunts - that of crossing the same sheet both latitudinally and longitudinally.' 'Come with me', he invites, 'and I will take you for the finest walk you ever had in your life, beginning on the Bosham creeks over the long strip of coast where the fields come right down to the sea, until at Brighton we walk along the high chalk cliffs to Eastbourne, and thence across the Pevensey Level to the glens of Hastings and the vast sand dunes near Dungeness; then we will walk the whole length of the close-cropped turf of the Downs from Eastbourne to Harting, descending to inspect each Downland village, after which we will trace every stream in the Weald from the Western to the Eastern Rother, by way of Arun, Adur, Ouse, Cuckmere and Brede; and in the end we will come to Horsham over the high, sandy ridge of the five forests of Ashdown, Balcombe, Tilgate, Worth and St. Leonards.'

Mais makes good his invitation in seven enjoyable chapters. In the preface to the book, he reveals his sources in a passage lauding his antecedents the Curwens, E.V. Lucas, Lady Wolseley and especially Rudyard Kipling, and acknowledging the volumes of *Sussex Archeological Collections*. He devotes two chapters each to the coast, the Downs and the Weald and a further chapter to the five forests. Each chapter describes the huge enjoyment he derived from the county, by means of an account of what he sees on his journey, with regular digressions into archaeology, history and literature, and frequent reference to cricket, and gives him an opportunity to air his passions, his personality and his prejudices. The book concludes with a useful critical bibliography, showing that he had read widely on the subject and had kept pace with recent archeological discoveries, many photographs, some of which he took himself, and maps of the six Sussex Rapes, but not before he returns again to his beloved Southwick in an extra chapter. After his arrival in Sussex, Mais seldom failed to mention the village in his many books, and the description of the Green from *All the Days of My Life*, written a little later in 1937, gives a taste of his full-bodied style:

> The Green was the centre of all our activities. It was here that the village cricket Eleven played on Wednesday evenings in the dim light and on Saturday afternoons. It was here that the village band played on Sundays after Evensong, that the children held their school sports, the folk dancers and gymnasts their displays, and the girls played Stoolball. It was here that the old men played out their days sitting on the benches in the sun with the dogs at their feet. It was here that the village boys and girls rode round and round in the evenings on their bicycles or stopped at the railings to flirt or gossip. It was here that cottage women would swiftly pass with jugs half-hidden under shawls to the *Cricketers Arms* and children race noisily to the sweetshop next door to get far more for their money than their money warranted from the white-haired gracious lady who owned it.
>
> It was here that the stout fishmonger with stentorian voice used to call his wares so loudly that I could hear him from the top of Thundersbarrow. It was here that small urchins squirted each other from the pump that commemorated Queen Victoria's Jubilee, and chased each other round the War Memorial. On certain days at half-past two there were the slow, sad processions of mourners and the beribboned cars of the newly married. All life passed before me as I read and wrote, the usual mingling quickly with the unusual, the rector going slowly blind, the headmaster with a strangely incongruous bowler walking quickly past so near the wall as almost to touch it, the young headmistress wobbling off her bicycle to ask if I had got this or that new book, a stranger hesitating at the garden-gate to ask where the church or harbour was. It was the one disadvantage of the Green that we couldn't see the sea.

We could only hear it, and sometimes smell what the polite call the ozone.

He was scarcely less lyrical about the sea at Southwick. 'But warm or cold we would go to the beach', he wrote - 'This entailed crossing the Brighton-Worthing railway line, and the main street, a very shoddy and dangerous thoroughfare. But beyond it rose the masts of many yachts drawn alongside Courtenay and Birkett's quay in the canal. To reach the sea we had to cross the canal over the lock-gates or by ferry, and there was always some activity to give us pause, a Scandinavian timber ship, a French potato-boat, a Dutch barge, a collier, an oil-tanker, or a little private yacht going in or out. And on the seaside of the canal was a strangely attractive wasteland where still stood the bases of those honeycombs like towers of concrete and iron that were to be towed out in mid-channel as observation posts for enemy submarines.

Water now flowed in and out among the hollow hexagons and anglers fished for dabs, and we kept an eagle eye open for the flash past of the deep red breast and sky-blue wings of the solitary kingfisher who held sway over this narrow channel. Wild flowers grew in fine profusion in the shingle, sea-pinks, viper's bugloss, and deadly nightshade. In winter when the weather was very severe the grey geese sought sanctuary here, but the gunmen soon got wind of stray wild duck and brent geese and their lives were short. This channel was spanned by a broken-down bridge and a dam built below the observation towers. Then came the camel's back of shingle on the other side of which dipped the shingle beach with groynes about seventy yards apart to hold the beach in place. The groynes provided us with admirable places on which to hang our clothes when we undressed, and even more admirable protection from the wind. The temptation to lie in the sun and let the world go by was overwhelming'.

Mais showed, in his series of post-war travel books, that he could write entertainingly in short simple sentences, but the nearer he came to his spiritual home, the more lyrical his writing became. He again describes Southwick, his actual as well as his spiritual home, in a separate chapter in his *Sussex*: 'Architecturally we have not much to show. Our main street, running parallel with the sea, is known to every motorist on his way between Brighton and Worthing, first, because he is compelled to go slowly through it, secondly because of its apparent drabness. "She is not fair to outward view as other maidens be.' It is only when you turn aside under the railway arch that the full glory of the Green, with the gentle slope and ribbed tilth of the multicoloured Downs behind, strikes you'.

Those who only know Southwick from driving along the main road, and have never turned under the railway arch, would never guess that here was the locale of *Esther Waters*; here was the place where John Cowper Powys decided to settle in Sussex, because the harbour made him think of Weymouth; here was the birthplace of Dr. Pell and Dame Clara Butt. 'Here', Mais continued, 'cattle grazed and chicken scratched and small boys fished for 'tiddlers' in a stream long since dead. Here the Engineers encamped while building those mystery ships that were to clear the bottom of the Channel from all hidden foes. Here, now swept and garnished, disfigured by no speck of paper or peel of orange, babies crawl, schoolgirls huddle, boys race, men play cricket, gossips dawdle, old men sing, and all the world is merry on the long summer evenings when the shadows of the western trees creep towards the cricket pitch. The houses that fringe it represent all modern stages of domestic architecture mainly in red brick. The only ones that have beauty are the chequered, knapped flint, seventeenth-century Hall, the thatched flint cottage, now a dairy, where Charles II is supposed to have rested on the last stage of his escape from Worcester, and the long flint-walled, thatched barn with the big tarred doors in the middle.'

There have been many books written on Sussex. They

overflow the shelves of the local studies collection in the Record Office or in the larger libraries scattered round the county, but few if any have been written with such enthusiasm, such passion and such love, and none in such masculine prose. All the editions of *Sussex* that I have seen are small enough to fit snugly in a jacket or coat pocket and, accompanied by the relevant Ordnance Survey map, are the perfect companions for the exploration of the county.

Note:
Mais's motto was to see England first before venturing abroad. 'For years I have walked alone over England', he wrote, and it was as well he did. His pace and stamina would have confounded most companions, even in the days before the motor car made walking the pastime of the discerning few. In *Oh! to be in England* he described a day's walk on the Lizard, which began in Helston, continued via Porthleven, along the coast to Mullion, across the Lizard peninsula to Poltesco, up the east coast along Kennack Sands, inland to St. Keverne and back to Helston again - a walk that my wife and I would have been proud to achieve in a week on our annual holiday in West Penwith. 'I have beaten records for time and distance,' he proudly boasted, but then added that he had seen nothing. 'It is only now that I am beginning to moderate my pace that I am beginning to see any of the colours and shapes and hear any of the music'. His travel books sold well, he became a well-known broadcaster, and as part of his work for the railways, he led week-end walks all over Southern England, collecting his companions at the railway station. For the Great Western Railway, he wrote two books - *Glorious Devon* and *The Cornish Riviera* - both in 1928, and for Southern Railway Company three - *Southern Rambles for Londoners, Walking at Weekends* and *Hills of the South* - consisting of descriptions of walks (all of which started at a railway station), coloured paintings and maps.

But his best book is *All the Days of My Life,* the first volume of his outspoken and enthusiastic autobiography. All his books, including his novels, were partly autobiographical, but in the first volume of his autobiography he simply writes about himself, his life and his opinions, and reveals the flavour of his character. In the book, he described his attitude to travel: 'My travelling has always been a child's game. I travel exactly as a child travels, full of expectancy, in continued astonishment, counting on everyone to do everything for me, totally ignorant of what I have to pay, totally ignorant of the languages that are being spoken all around me, fearful of danger, grotesquely uncomfortable, but enjoying every moment of it'. Mais was obviously not a conventional travel writer. He travelled accompanied by his second wife, Jill, and their two daughters, Lalage and Imogen; they usually travelled by public transport and they seldom had much money. He was the first chronicler of package holidays and coach tours, and wrote informal accurate practical guides to the new world of post-war holidays, filled with detailed prices, enthusiastic descriptions of food and drink and a great deal of his happy family life.

In *I return to Switzerland* in 1948 he hit upon the diary form, and henceforth his travel books were written as family diaries, in a characteristic mixture of informality and accuracy. Descriptions of family packing, sea-board sickness, and quarrels over glasses of passion fruit were interspersed with detailed costings of financial transactions at banks and customs, lists of prices for hotels, boarding houses and excursions, and specific recommendations for food and drink. 'Leaving Capri was certainly and adventure', he wrote in *Italian Holiday* - one of his very last travel books - 'In the first place it took us all day to leave. It is true that we spent much time in the morning in the shops as Jill suddenly decided that she wanted a bathing suit, but again we found the cost prohibitive. I think 10,000 lire a little absurd for a bathing suit. That gives you some idea of what the tourist may expect in high summer in Capri. I got our bill for ten days stay. It came to 84,000 lire for the three of us. That works out at about £5 a day. Obviously at this rate no English family can afford to stay in Capri for more than a few days. In any event it is much too crowded and much too hot in August. None-the-less there is no question that it is the most colourful and exotic island that I have ever visited'.

I have met people who take Mais's books with them and deliberately visit the places he visited, stay in the hotels where the family stayed, and enjoy the excursions that he recommended. After Scotland, the family visited the rest of the British Isles, the Riviera, Norway and the Isle of Man for Christopher Johnson, and Madeira, the Alps, Austria, Italy, Spain, Majorca and Holland for Alvin Redman; then they enjoyed cruises in the Mediterranean, the Caribbean and around South America, and they ventured as far as Africa, Greece and finally round the World. And always the reader was left in no doubt as to what to expect.

'Before you start fingering that 12s 6d or 15s or whatever it is the publisher and bookseller wish you to pay for this book, I should like you to know what sort of a book it is', he wrote in *Winter Sports Holiday* in 1951. 'It is emphatically not a technical guide to skiing. It is true that I passed my Third-Class test in 1922. It is true that I was the only skier to fall off the ski-lift from the Hornberg to the Hornflush and certainly the only skier in living memory to descend the Hornberg by a series of kick-turns, a fashion that died with Queen Victoria; but . . . ' In a sense he continued to play the xenophobic Englishman. Mais was not a man to seek out and explore the remote and the exotic. He chose the tried and familiar, the places where he met his fellow-countrymen, and he saw them and described them from an English point of view. Nor were the holidays always a success. Writing in *Norwegian Holiday*, the same year, he complained: 'Norway isn't tourist minded. There's nothing to drink. It's expensive. The people seldom smile. The mountains and fjords are terrific, and that's about all there is to be said about it.' Mais's post-war travel books were written in diary form in hotel rooms after the day's excursions, and describe in short sentences all that the family had experienced. They reflect the gradual opening up of Europe and the wider world after the war and the immediate post-war shortages. They were written for the ordinary tourist, and their popularity shows how successful he was in reflecting their needs and aspirations.

TWENTY-SEVEN

Strange Meetings: Sculpture at Goodwood

John Saunders

Had it not been for Jumbo, I might never have visited Sculpture at Goodwood. Somehow I never get round to visiting local tourist attractions. So, I suppose, I should be grateful to Jumbo, even though I had little sympathy for him in his melancholic mood. We had spent the morning visiting West Sussex sites of natural and architectural beauty. A winding drive across the downs, with its spring-fresh greenery and its lakes of linseed blue, had left him quite unmoved, as did our walk through Kingley Vale and our look at Goodwood House. Jumbo remained coldly morose, wilfully locked in the immediate past. That is until we visited Sculpture at Goodwood.

Sculpture at Goodwood is the home, the temporary home, of a shifting collection of some forty or more modern sculptures. It is set in Hat Hill Copse within grounds of the permanent home of Wilfred and Jeannette Cass who have devoted the last five years to commissioning, showing and selling contemporary British sculpture. Every year twelve or so new pieces are commissioned. Visitors may, for ten pounds, stroll through the copse on the Goodwood estate where they will have a number of strange encounters with our modernist legacy. The better-off visitors may, if they so wish, go on to purchase something from the collection. My old friend Jumbo was neither wealthy, nor a modernist. Until the day of our visit, his cultural values had been securely Victorian - accepting a combination of patriarchy and

Sculpture at Goodwood

STRANGER III (1959 - cast in 1996)
Lynn Chadmick

utilitarianism as both natural and God-given.

Jumbo's metamorphosis began with his encounter with *Stranger III*. It was, indeed, a strange meeting, as the certainties of the nineteenth century came into collision with the ambiguities of the twentieth. Stranger, some eight feet high, stands on three legs in a small glade where three paths meet. My initial impression was of a sort of dragon- fish, designed by Lowry. Jumbo gazed mournfully at it and then consulted the 'Guide', provided free with his ticket. I, too, consulted my copy. Then melancholy gave way to anger. 'What! No. That can't be. Half a million. Five hundred thousand pounds. That's over five million rand - for that?' Jumbo's well-clipped South African accent threatened to deconstruct. 'It's by Lynn Chadwick', I said, knowingly. 'She's quite well known. It's probably a collector's piece.' 'Five million rand'. It was the final proof for Jumbo that the world had grown mad. 'Do you call that Art?' he asked accusingly. 'Well, yes', I said, vaguely aware that my answer was indebted to a similar moment of confrontation in D.H. Lawrence's *Women in Love*. 'It is Art because...because it hints at truths about the human condition.' *Stranger III* leered at me out of its right eye. 'It's...it's part dinosaur, part insect, part tank. It roots us in evolution, hinting at our potential for both growth and wanton destruction. It...' *Stranger III* leered at Jumbo out of its other eye and I realized that from where I was standing Stranger was at least in part elephant and that Jumbo had found himself gazing into a mirror, a satirical mirror. He was silent. We moved on. Later that night, having discovered the Sculpture at Goodwood internet site (www.sculpture.org.uk), I learned a little more about Lynn Chadwick and *Stranger III*. The original had been commissioned in 1956 by the Air League of the British Empire to commemorate the double crossing of the Atlantic by the Airship R 34 in July 1919. It was to have been positioned outside the Long Haul Terminal at Heathrow Airport. However, in 1958, a committee led by Lord Brabazon of Tara with the support of the Guild of Air Pilots and Aviators forced the Air League to withdraw their commission. Lord Brabazon is said to have dismissed the work as 'a diseased haddock'. And, oh yes, Lynn Chadwick was unambiguously male!

The walk through Hat Hill Copse takes the form of an unguided tour. Metal markers, like yellow snakes, show the way. We sauntered on becoming more and more aware of the play of light and the twitter of bird song. Though there had been several cars in the car park, we seemed to be alone in the forest. The sky darkened as the next sculpture loomed into view. It was another enigma. Some twenty feet high, it seemed at first to be a temple, then a rocket, then a time-machine, then a combination of all three. 'It's called Druva Mystery', Jumbo announced. It glowed in the gloom with an unnatural, other-worldly green. 'Could it be kryptonite?' I wondered, peering at my 'Guide'. 'No', I corrected Jumbo, 'it's by Dhruva Mistry. It's called *The Object* and it's made of stainless steel.' 'Then why is it worth only £40,000?' Jumbo demanded, struck by what seemed blatant unfairness. But the hint of a religious mystery had left him treading somewhat warily and, after inspecting *The Object* from all sides, we again moved on.

The woods were lovely dark and deep and gradually the magic of the setting began to enchant us both. We came upon a giant head and, bonded by the same school anthology, said in unison, 'My name is Ozymandius King of Kings'. It was, in fact, *Head* by John Davies. Head was not a kingly head with a sneer of cold command. It was somewhat pock-marked and what seemed like cigarette ends were coming out of its mouth and its nose and its eyes. Next came two much frailer figures by Nicola Hicks. We identified them easily enough as a podgy Little Red Riding Hood and an all-knowing, rather enigmatic Wolf, who gazed at his potential prey down a long thin snout. 'Was it a Grandmother in a mask, or a Wolf in Grandmother's clothing?' I wondered. For a moment I enjoyed the sense that I was in a kind of sculptural Disney Land, sharing the way with figures taken from fairy tales. But there was something disconcerting about the image and its title - *Recovered Memory*.

Though cast in bronze, the figures seemed to be made out of something much less durable - straw and clay, perhaps. What is more, the texture suggested disintegration or decay and I had the disconcerting impression that they were incomplete relics torn from the past, torn perhaps from a hidden corner of my own brain. It was only when revisiting the images on the internet that I realized that these impressions were not arbitrary. The internet commentary suggests that

Sculpture at Goodwood

RECOVERED MEMORY (1997)
Nicola Hicks

the two figures evoke both a disconcerting realisation of the potentially sinister significance of traditional fairy tales and, as indirectly suggested in the title, a horrendous realisation of real or imagined childhood trauma. Jumbo was - at this point - locked again in his own immediate past, re-living a painful memory.

Jumbo Fourie, a friend of my youth, had arrived triumphantly in Chichester two days earlier. A lifetime of stay-at-home parsimony had been undone by a moment of madness, a sudden surrender to cricket fever. South Africa's seemingly irresistible progress through the 1999 World Cup had seduced him into taking advantage of a cheap return flight to London and a not-so-cheap black market ticket for the final at Lords. But, alas! We had together watched the Thursday semi-final, that titanic struggle which had ended in a run-out and a tie and the South African team's hasty return to Johannesburg. And Jumbo, now quite uninterested in the final, found himself with the best part of a week to spend before his own return. His rash venture - he kept telling us - had cost him 'more than ten thousand rand'. I could see by the pain on his face that he was yet again re-experiencing that fatal run-out.

The twittering of the birds began to give way to a ruder, more insistent sound. Somewhere ahead there seemed to be a perturbation in nature. Wild geese? The cry of sea gulls? We spent a moment enjoying George Cutt's *Reflections*, two shimmering, spiralling, glistening pillars mounted on what turned out to be a motorised plinth. There was a silver globe on one of the pillars that reflected the sky and the surrounding copse. And then we came to the source of the commotion. Walls of Sound by William Furlong consists of two giant sound boxes, a sort of symplegades which drew us into a narrow corridor of steel. Each sound box seemed to have been programmed to convey a range of natural harmonious sound - water, birds, bees. As we entered we seemed to trigger a new discordancy. The corridor became a

Hitchcockian world where birds screamed and slashed - a kind of vernal Psycho.

We made our way along the eastern wall of the Park where we encountered Jumbo's second alter ego. Behind a tree, something unambiguously elephant was leaping out of what looked like a striped hat box. 'A kind of Jack-in-the-Box,' I thought. 'Ach, man!' said Jumbo with the delighted recognition of one remembering a favourite aunt, 'It's Nellie. It's Nellie the Elephant. You know…'. And with a voice which had not sung for a long time, he croaked the refrain, 'Nellie the Elephant packed her trunk and said goodbye to the Circus'. And, suddenly the hat box became a child's memory of a Circus Tent, as Nellie sprang into the jungle forest. 'It's called *Another Surprise for Fabricius Luscinus*, I said, dampening Jumbo's enthusiasm with a little learning easily acquired from the Guide. 'Fabrish who?' he asked disappointedly. We were, I later learned, both right. Here was an example of the postmodernist's delight in double-coding. For the child in us all the sculpture is and will always be Nellie. In fact, it was only after it had been constructed that the sculptor, Jim Unsworth, discovered the story of Fabricius and bestowed on his creation its grander title, a title derived from Plutarch who tells how during the Punic Wars, Pyrrhus, the King of Epirus, attempted to terrify a prisoner, Fabricius, by hiding an elephant in a tent and letting the animal burst out in front of him. The stoical

Sculpture at Goodwood

ANOTHER SURPRISE FOR
FABRICIUS LUSCINUS (1998)
Jim Unsworth

Fabricius stood his ground. The internet commentary reminds its readers that for the purist this creation is neither Nellie nor Fabricius, but form, pure form, 'a craggy, lumpen form escaping containment'.

We passed a stagnant pond. Or was it a pond? There was no mention of it in the 'Guide'. Then we came to Bill Woodrow's *Endeavour*, a giant black cannon, cast in bronze, which stands boldly on the southern boundary of the park. That afternoon it appeared to be aimed menacingly at a herd of nonchalant cattle in the adjoining field. The 'Guide' provided us with its full title: *Endeavour: Cannon Dredged from the First Wreck of the Ship of Fools*. On closer inspection we realized that here was no ordinary simulacrum of a cannon but, with books and musical instruments for wheels and other emblematical features, a weighty, satirical, multi-coded sermon on human folly and the folly of war.

Sculpture at Goodwood

MISS PRISM (1998)
William Pye

191

(The internet site provides a plausible reading.)

Next we came to the image which I would most like to own, to have in my own garden. William Pye's *Miss Prism* is a shimmering, water-glistening, three-sided, fifteen foot high, rectilinear construction made of highly polished steel. Beneath the steel form there appears to be a motor which is finely tuned to pump water through the top of the prism so that it cascades down the sides in a fine film. As we approached, we became aware of the sound of echoing water, reminiscent of the gurgling of a spring. 'Why call it *Miss Prism*?' asked Jumbo, now somewhat cowed by my displays of learning. 'I'm not sure', I answered. 'It's probably just a play on words, combining a reference to its prismatic form with the idea of pristine, virginal primness, and referring amusedly to the Miss Prism in *The Importance of Being Earnest*.' As we circled the construction the sun emerged from behind a cloud and we could see our own far from pristine images reflected in the tracery of the water. 'When I get back I must go on a diet,' announced Jumbo, 'you people are feeding me too well'. I looked at his image. The face appeared to be almost smiling.

We passed what seemed at first a giant intestine, *Mother Tongue*. We sat for a moment in a small rural amphitheatre, dominated by a strange two-dimensional bronze construction, part human, part animated history. And then we came to the work that finally broke Jumbo's resistance.

In a clearing on the edge of the copse was a shipwreck in the sky. Some eighty or more whitish granite columns of irregular height gave the impression of a gigantic wave. Attached to the columns, so that they seemed to be resting on the horizon above the copse beyond, were two boat-shaped stones or stone-shaped boats. Here, in this skyward graveyard, was a hint of immortality. I felt like stout Cortez! The sculptor, Stephen Cox (the internet tells us), had visited India in 1985 and had stayed in Mahabalipuram, a coastal village known for its expertise in temple carving. For several months he had worked with the Indian carvers, becoming increasingly interested in the distinctive village fishing boats which he had observed both beached and at sea. Later he had bought several boats, which he had housed in his studio, sensing that one day they would become the subject of a composition. In 1994 *Granite Catamarans on a Granite Wave*, commissioned by the Hat Hill Sculpture Foundation, was realized. Together, we gazed in awe, experiencing a moment *sub specie aeternitatis*. The world cup defeat became just a memory of a moment lost in time.

Looking back on that afternoon, my final image will be of our exit from the park. As we left the gallery and walked towards the car park, there, dancing beneath the trees on the skyline, were a pair of gigantic pachyderms. Were they hippos or elephants? We couldn't tell. In place of heads they had great guffawing mouths which resembled gigantic tubas or the loud speakers of old fashioned gramophones. These great mouth shapes gave the impression that they were both creating the music for their dance and laughing hilariously at their own absurdity. Were they hippos or elephants? Probably the former. According to www.sculpture.org uk, the sculptor (a South African, Steven Gregory) thinks that the image came to him after watching a television wildlife programme about the hippopotamus. We, of course, did not then know this but the 'Guide' did tell us the name of the sculpture: *The Two of Us Together*. I looked at Jumbo. Jumbo looked at me. We had both been slender, once. There was another moment of recognition.

I could see that he was thinking, 'rather like a hippo'. His face broke into a gigantic grin. 'Shall we dance?' he suggested. And arm in arm we walked to the car.

Sculpture at Goodwood

THE TWO OF US (1998)
Steven Gregory

TWENTY-EIGHT

Jane German: *Cow and Calf: Evening at East Head (1999)*

An oil painting of beasts on flat land near the sea (West Wittering) in the slanting light of evening.

   Countryside work, and farm animals, precisely and lovingly observed, are part of a tradition which flourished in the nineteenth and early twentieth centuries with painters like Clausen, Stanhope Forbes, Edward Scott (who worked locally around Arundel), and the great and neglected Harry Becker in East Anglia. These painters were spurred on by both the precursors of Impressionism and by Impressionism itself, but they also look back to the Dutch masters of the seventeenth century in their celebration of the everyday life of work and husbandry.

TWENTY-NINE

BETWEEN TWO WORLDS

Richard Williamson

There is no difficulty in imagining, as Chesterton did, that the moon was blood. I sit on the beach at Pagham in the autumn night, and there is nobody else there. Most would think this a hostile place in the cold and blank darkness, the groynes and pebbles with only one, seen, silvered side, the water heaving and black but freckled with ten thousand shifting, winking lights. The sea grinds the pebbles, they sigh and roll over; the sea is reforming them for another journey. Soon they will be covered for six hours as the tide advances. Underwater, I listen to their calls, which are deeper, slower, less urgent. I take a handful and feel their moon shape. The tide is flooding through the bank now, racing like a Scottish salmon river, feeling the muds of Pagham harbour, feeding crabs and flatfish and cockles which have become hungry in the past six hours.

The moon has brought them food. At some unimaginably distant time, tutored and in harmony with the sun, the moon gave earth's oceans their heartbeat. A long, everlasting, relaxed and confident stride of movement which brought up the waters for their six hour intake, and then their six hour exhale. Like a vast white egg the moon looks on the night - 'in delight', as Blake remarked. In its early time it too was molten, red, with the first feelings of its own embryo developing. But it fostered instead the oceans of the earth.

The autumn night is warm. Phosphorescence shines around my body like an electric current as I swim. Sand eels wriggle underneath, blobs of sea wrack are like small towns seen from an airliner, their life busy and travelling within themselves on urgent, unknown adventures. A crab ponders the sea bed, and fiddles with strands of seaweed, handing pieces to its mouth. There are shrimps down there whose whole existences are transparent with the light of the sea, all seeing light. Diatoms and sprat of limpet journey past in their thousand, perhaps on the only journey of their lives, but with eternity as their intent.

The sea is blood, the channels veins. The harbour breathes in. To its far reaches, worms wait, even against the walls, and a million snails slide slowly out among the spartina stems. Winkles lift their doors, and walk beneath the waters, tasting soft food. Ragworms suck the salt, browse fields of mud in underwater deliberation, chewing tiny things whose journey then is done. After hours, when water pressure slackens and tells the worm its table will be cleared, it travels down into its own wet secret hole and through the U-bend of its whole existence makes a coiled pyramid in satisfaction. The sea moves on again, taking travellers onwards to another place. It slides like a tongue along the bank, murmuring its greetings and memories of times past among the stones. There are the ancient memories inside each pebble of life, locked and gone. The sea remembers, the stones speak, and tell of that other time. Here is a shark's tooth, there a sponge, nearby the relic of a sea urchin, all frozen in flint. The moon tells how once it drew tides like milk, white and languorous in tropic heat, when this dense milt of life settled slowly into beds of chalk and slumbered for eighty million years, until woken again one day along the cliffs for another journey.

Where to now? The pebbles are impatient. But they must wait longer than the chalk, which has quickly made itself into living skeletons of plaice and Dover sole. So the stones shout and cheer in storms, rolling frenziedly up and down the banks of Pagham, grinding themselves together in a froth, greeting the giant ocean's grip, longing for freedom to live again, tired of their ancient mariner's tales of that other life of long ago. Onwards to the next, free us! Break us and pound us to bits! Let the sea in and over Selsey, we won't stop it. Let us suck the sea again and feel the moon's heart carrying us on to other places, to a tropic sea again, to grow in coral or a monster's eye.

Over the glass-glint brittle-break of moonlight I can see other travellers in this night over the sea. Are they beams of light, or birds in flight? The silly conundrum baffles me momentarily. Some parts move so fast, others seem to flick on and off and stay in one place. The binoculars reveal what is happening. A flock of avocets has arrived in the night, black and white as the light. It is a riddle of waves and hollows and flickering wings. They fly on over the pebble and settle in the moonlight in the muds behind and stand there like new flints broken open, their travels from a cretaceous time achieved, their new life black and white again but this time flying, flying! We crawled out of the sea once, Caliban and scaly, staring at the sky in wonder. The sea drains away, leaving the pebbles immobile and soundless, though eager even at my footsteps to rattle and rebel and shake themselves free a little more.

Curlews remember the moors, and trail trills of bubble songs linked into chains across the harbour. They are travellers from distance, careless with their songs from Lapland that they drop into the Sussex night, stirring longings in people lying below in their lonely beds, watching their lives go by. It is the song of the midnight sun swinging through the empty half of the world, of wild geese and reindeer.

But there is another tale to be told here on the pebble ridge as I sit in the warm September night, which also comes from a long curved beak like the curlew's. It is a tale of a small black seed that fell among the stones two years ago and struggled back up again until it felt the sea's spray. Then it opened its first soft downy leaf into the spring. Two years passed among the tramp of feet as people walked the beach, and dogs and foxes wandered, searching for places to tell each other the news as this yellow poppy by the sea survived and finally opened its crinkled flag of petals. Bees from the shore found it and paid it for its pollen by moving on, and the flower slowly became a long curving beak of equal shape as of the curlew. Autumn days have two songs of longing, of opiate and the country green.

So onwards, like the sea and the falling moon, and the wind which whispers of its journeys, and the restless birds. Past Selsey, that Achilles' heel of Sussex. On to the daylight. This is a boundary march the Romans never knew, nor did their sea for it was yet a mile to the south.

PAGHAM HARBOUR

It is low tide, and midday heat shakes the dry sea bed. Is that a piece of paper or a tiny shore bird? The sky inverts itself briefly onto the sand and makes the figment of a pool and wobbles back again. White sails flutter out to sea, unmoving, shredded by strokes of sun, hardly moved by breeze. There is a softness, a warmth, in the mouth of Chichester harbour. It kissed the moon-tides a million times, sucking her breast, swallowing the chalks and clays of Wight, growing fat on the produce of her streams until her veins are choked, her body soft and stuffed with food. Men once walked across her, using pattens, copying the birds. Now they have forgotten how. The muds wheeze and sigh and breathe with tiny lives, some say ten thousand in a pint. Birds swarm here like sky shoals of fish, flicking this way and that, a thousand white undersides in a second, in the next, all lost in grey.

People swarm, too, pink bellies burning among the pink of thrift and bindweed. Flowers swarm on the littoral, galaxies of milkwort that open briefly in the spring and close before they're noticed. There are ninety different species in the East Head sandhills alone. Sea lavenders make a skyful of blue on July muds; sea heath is a tide-mark of matted plants in a sandy hollow, its mauve, crinkled petals no bigger than the smallest snail.

Ring plovers lay eggs to the grieving envy of small stones, pointed to the centre, and sometimes they escape the urban dogs, and then eggs turn into soft warm freckled grey which lie still. A great heat settles in the September hollows, the sand purrs but burns like hot glass. Small bees struggle with pollen to solitary burrows. The skylark's song dries up like a shed skin, its daily column shrivels and fades from the mind. The sun drew up blood in spring, boils it away by autumn. The dunes swoon like the dreaming Sphinx and are content as they live through this change of life. They came down from the hills, from the dead beds of chalk and were turned out of that estuary into a sudden alteration by the sea as it played with its waves and caught them unawares and gave them a new nobility. All the time, as the brief span of Man pompously alters the surface of things the sea is making different plans with the sky. Shall it freeze itself for awhile like mad red Mars, and cease all life for a billion years? Meanwhile it will try new forms of life here in the new sea beds. It might decide to rise and nibble the chalk hills again and leave its beach mark to puzzle whatever intelligence that may one day come again.

Now and then it will drown a child or break a boat. Often

it feels sullen with the foul dumped waste it has to suck in its mouth. But at high tide here in this harbour the sea will often give a dark blue hour of rest near East Head, gold-lined by the sun along wave edge and ripple, a contemplative depth that is the mind of the ocean. In winter this moment of rest turns the water almost black, and sea ducks dive, and bob back as gleaming white as chalk.

September is the best time, as flowers remain while arctic travellers arrive. It is then I hear the crake-call of the Sandwich tern, that ancient mariner which will soon be south with the albatross beyond the equator. It is the lament that haunts: it is the cry of drowned sailors. It is the dirge of the fado song which tells longingly of death, and the inevitable return to rebirth. The crake splits the calm September day as a wedge rives oak: the weakest place. It is the invisible sound of disaster, as fishermen once feared Orca the Gladiator and his urgent surge of intent. It is like the croak of the Danish crow in East Anglia, flying in with the Vikings with their silent dipping oars and sun-burnished shields. I lie in the sandhills glad that today's brilliant sun can mock all such black monarchs of the night.

But September's easeful days pass. The moons ride the nights higher and yet higher; the sun falls day by day and hides in clouds; far away, unheard here, the cry of wild geese telling that the sun has died, that they are flying before a storm, travelling across half the world.

Then one day a wolf wind with the race memory of a glacier pours down from the hills. Lapwings flee in thousands, line upon line across the evening sky to France. Ten thousand Brent geese huddle into creek crevices gabbling in fear, knowing how the sea can freeze, how star-glitter on water can dull suddenly like dead eyes.

Waves slush languidly on the pebble ridge of Pagham. The harbour becomes a white sea, with gliding floes like swans. Among them a dozen smews hide and seek, white as ice, thin black lines of shadow lines criss-crossed as cracks. Other strange birds arrive: scaups and eiders, great northern divers, patrolling with their necks alert as periscopes. On Pilsey sands thirty thousand dunlin huddle in sleep, the wind gnawing their bones. At low tide they feed fearfully, knowing how beaks can freeze into mud. The wind shrieks in the dunes, making mock sun dials with thrashing marram grass. Teal flight to East Head's frozen rain pools, hoping for fresh water, pipits crouch in terror under dune lee.

Sand and snow entwine, forming the shapes of a new order, reminders of what they could achieve. By night the hurtling sky, bringing black snow like lemmings fleeing into darkness. By day a sun shrunk with age, blood red, one day dying, one day fading far and cold, its journey done.

THIRTY

MY CONSTITUTIONAL: ALONG ALDWICK BAY

Spencer Thomas

Down the lane, past the coastguards' cottages and the site of the Napoleonic Barracks which identifies it, to the point where, if continued, it would converge with Dark Lane and Sea Lane at the tithing of Charlton, reputedly the victim of coastal erosion: the lanes themselves have been cut off at the knees leaving their feet paddling in the lost village submerged under Aldwick Bay, but within five minutes urbanism evaporates as a coastal world beckons me to spend a couple of hours in its company.

The route is identical each day but the scene is always different for the interface between land and sea is constantly changing in response to the elements. The smooth, inclined profile produced in calm conditions is contorted by winter storms into a roller coaster of vertical drops and swooping curves. In spring and autumn the rhythmic ebb and flow of the tide moulds the precipitous edges into ergonomic excesses, and observation over successive days charts the transition from hard walls of rolled pebbles into soft caresses of slumping stones.

Persistent nudging by the sea, with a little help from gravity, gradually teases the shore into a succession of suggestive shapes imitating a sculptor patiently chiselling to produce the desired figure. The vertical cliff is first scoured into a maze of miniature bays and headlands that are progressively refined into croissant-coiffured cusps resembling the open jaws of a pincers. These armchair-shaped hollows sit facing the approaching sea anticipating the next incursion, like a recumbent female enticing a lover. The progress is serene and certain until the hollow is full and the water rolls along the lip until it withdraws to regain strength in preparation for its next penetration. This process of advance and retreat creates a perfectly regular series of graded cusps that reinvent themselves, as if a giant automated press had stamped its way along the beach.

At other times an escalator is sculpted into the shingle, the stones seeming to have been ironed into a cascade of level shelves connected by steep steps. The analogy with inundations in past geological epochs when hills

Above and below
TWO VIEWS OF BEACH CUSPS,
Aldwick Bay (1981)

and mountains were planed during rises and falls in the relative height of land and sea is inescapable. Major tectonic events and forces which occurred over millions of years are replicated at a manageable scale on a daily basis - within a stone's throw of daily living, and walking.

The sheer symmetry, shimmering in the summer sun or squinting through the transparent gauze of an autumn mist, can be disturbed by a night of violence. Turbulent waves crashing on the shelving shore replicate a predatory hammer striking the anvil, biting into the surface to re-sort the material for a fresh start. Perfection is replaced by chaos. The path from genesis to exodus is strewn with the flotsam of hope and despair, faith and doubt, insight and ignorance but with the certainty that out of the confusion a new form will emerge bearing the hand of the maker.

The daily journey along the beach is uninterrupted when the pebbles have been swept into a homogeneous whole by the giant brush of the previous tide, but more hazardous when the currents have mixed the ingredients in the bowl and cooked up recognizable shapes: vandal currents engage in the thuggery of disturbance and disruption while their conformist cousins advocate a policy of avoidance and retention of the artist's conception. Respect and admiration for the composition require the walker to tip-toe and, to preserve its pristine condition, take detours. Fronds of green sea cabbage draw a tide mark around the neck of the bay, framing the picture in a surgical collar. Gull choirs congregating for rehearsal and screeching arias to approaching strangers provide another obstacle. Their behaviour mirrors human nature as they play chicken. The nervous fly away at the first scent of danger, whereas the mass of camp followers hold their ground as long as possible in a vain show of bravado, attempting to deter the intruder. The brave, nonchalant and laid back, only give way at the very last moment as the sound of crunching pebbles underfoot reverberate with the staccato of machine gun fire. The sleek-beaked, grey-backed, perpendicular pipe-legged sentries of the rocks resume their statuesque pose and reassert their rights after the danger has passed. They own the rusted, crusted outfall pipe which ejaculates like the rigid, gnarled penis it resembles.

The hunch-backed, oil-skinned, welly-legged fishermen huddle in their tents like Inuits in their bivouacs. The straining rod is firmly anchored in the shingle, slinging the arching line like a sliver of a disintegrating cobweb clinging to a twig - a slippery eel dancing like a dervish in an abortive attempt to regain freedom. An armour-plated crab trundling on the bottom of the bucket pretends to be a tank but will soon be on a dinner table. Tarred and feathered, lattice-windowed, bell-shaped lobster pots ring a peel to mourn the capture of a crustacean. Grey-scaled, pot-bellied, one-eyed mackerel wink their last good-byes on the marble slab - a fishy, molluscan mortuary.

The mood of the sea reflects the lie of the land and sways the emotions of the walker. The biting wind slices the spray off the surface of the waves sending a hissing, spitting curtain, showering into the sea in imitation of a chef producing a waterfall of pastry when trimming a tart around the edge of a plate. On a calmer day, the tide makes land with a final thrust, propelling the water up the slope like a frothing head of Guinness; procession of white horses piggy back across the bucking sea like salmon leaping to reach the first rung of the ladder, and the low angle of a dissipated, tired sun plays on the creased surface, blinding the onlooker who dares to peep; and the waves, as they roll up the beach, ever-increase their concavity of invitation until their support vanishes and they reluctantly collapse in a crumpled heap before the cycle of mating is complete.

The pebbles are graded like the grains of flour in the advertisement. The larger, heavier ones occupy the upper levels, having been hurled there by the high tides of winter storms, while the smaller grit hugs the water's edge. The rough edges have been knocked off as they rub against each other in their twice-daily grind up and down the beach. The deep holes in some stones, drilled by an invisible hand, are waiting to be filled with an amalgam of silt. Fleetingly, the stones part to reveal a tantalising glimpse of the golden sand they obscure, and ease the strain on the soles of shoes which feel as if they have been skating on ball bearings.

A kaleidoscope of shapes, sizes and colours: the whites, browns and blacks are readily identifiable as chalk, sandstone and flint, but where have the others come from? The source of the material is the projecting snout of the Manhood Peninsula which drips into the channel at Selsey Bill and is being relentlessly eroded. Beyond, the silhouette of the Isle of Wight hides in the hazy distance.

Spencer Thomas

ALDWICK BAY
*looking west towards
Selsey (1989)*

The prevailing winds and currents move the material longitudinally from west to east, depositing it along the pacific curve of Aldwick Bay. But this fails to explain the presence of the red and mottled pebbles dotting the beach. Have they well travelled from further afield and, being exhausted, accepted this as their final resting place? Are they invaders from across the channel, colonising the cemetery waiting for resurrection day when they will coerce the natives to join EMU? Have they been dredged up from the depths to reveal secrets of former epochs? Thoughts and questions and the search for answers lubricate the journey, but the revelation only comes at the end.

Springs gush from beneath the shingle, carving miniature valleys in the sand. Meanders shift and shuffle along the course of the river and braid like tracery in the delta as they slow. The flow tank in the laboratory is obsolete. The continuously evolving patterns simulate reality, albeit at a lilliputian scale. Metal detectors hoover the beach in search of treasure, but only divine tin cans. Oysters have left their flaky, pearly bodies behind, raided by aphrodisiacs searching for the elixir before Viagra. Sombrero-shaped shells siesta in the sinking sand. A helpless gull, wrapped in a black envelope of oily waste posted from the horizon, is delivered drowned. Slothful skippers shamelessly empty their tanks in the Channel entombing innocent victims in shrouds of sickening slime.

The backdrop to the walk comprises homes built as close to the shore as greed and boundaries allow. The price of sea views is high and might be higher if global warming raises sea level as forecast. The imposing 'stately homes' fringing the shore are, or were, permanent or temporary dwellings of royalty, pop stars, celebrities, tycoons, executives, and other well-heeled residents. The gated entrance declares the planned estate private to visitors who are advised to 'Keep out!' The brain wave of a property developer in the 1920s it has cultivated a manicured appearance and a status commensurate with the lofty ambitions advertised in the original prospectus, 'away from trippers, charabancs, bands, pierrot parties, noise and hustle'.

Ostentatious affluence comes to an abrupt end as it is replaced by the uniformed ranks of low-rise properties punctuated by post-modern constructions with towers, resembling periscopes, with portholes at second floor level straining to climb above the bungalows and furnish inland dwellings with desirable sea views. A little further and another sharp divide introduces a disorderly makeshift landscape variously described as an 'eyesore', 'an appalling spectacle', 'a hideous settlement', or a 'shanty town'. Unconventional curved roofs, elongated sides, narrow widths, modest heights, Play School windows, all give Sherlock Homes or Maigret, or one of the more recent T.V. sleuths or groups such as Time Team or House Detectives, the clues. Closer investigation and attention to the words etched on the windows, such as 'Smoking' or 'No smoking', reveals the origins in railway carriages. First class or third class coaches from S.R., L.M.S., L.N.E.R., and G.W.R. affirm dates from before nationalisation and British Rail and the onset of second class travel. Is this the graveyard or the dumping ground of pensioned-off stock, an early example of fly tipping? Or is it the end of the line for a disused station where entrepreneurs seized their opportunity to board abandoned carriages and transported them to their present positions? Or perhaps it is the fantasy of artistic licence where explorers decided to plant a colony at the extremity of civilised living?

The reality is more mundane but nonetheless entrepreneurial. Some years before the private estate was developed, cyclists and campers, having been attracted to the seaside on 2/6d day return rail excursions from Croydon and Guildford, and propaganda about sea air being good for health, purchased redundant carriages and transported them to Pagham on lorries. A wilderness of pebbles invited habitation, and the pioneers squatted on the top of the shingle ridge, in prime positions, to command an imposing view over the bay. 'The Shack', 'The Barn', 'L'Estrange', 'The Limit', 'The Outpost', testify eloquently to the ramshackle appearance of the structures, unmade roads, the absence of services and the remoteness and isolation of Pagham Beach nearly 100 years ago. Plotland culture was an initiative by people on marginal incomes acquiring places in the sun on marginal land, and

RAILWAY CARRIAGE
Pagham Beach (1999)

expressing their libertarian-ideals. It was their Arcadia.

Fashions and bureaucracy change and to the County Council the area represented A Rocky Horror Show. Attempts to blitz this negation of planning failed, but a policy of permitting owners to improve their properties and move upmarket had the desired effect by converting the 'raffishly picturesque' into an imitation of everywhere else. Happily the tradition of freedom, individuality, and spontaneity survives as haciendas and villas sit alongside ubiquitous bungalows. However, the parable is being ignored despite the foundations resting on shifting sands.

The terminus is reached. Pagham Harbour is an exaggeration but not a misnomer. Medieval trade with France once exchanged wool and corn for wine, loaded and landed at Sidlesham and Pagham. Silting killed the trade but produced rich land encouraging reclamation for agriculture. The 1910 storm finally restored it to its natural state. The mud flats are a nationally renowned Nature Reserve, functioning as a lay-by and service station for over-wintering geese on their migratory journeys and a paradise for the trilby-hatted, Barbour-coated, binocular-eyed brigade of 'twitchers' who make regular sorties to spy transient species.

A breach in the shingle spit, which joined Selsey to Bognor like an umbilical cord, is now kept open artificially with massive retaining iron walls. The harbour is washed twice daily as the tide funnels into and out of the confined opening that doubles as an entrance and exit. The harbour is a safety valve that has been plumbed with an overflow tap to be opened to receive the Lavant each time Chichester is threatened with flooding.

Aldwick - The Old Vic - a theatre of Scandinavian dreams with a cast of billions of primeval, peripatetic pebbles producing a perpetually pulsating 'Son et Lumiere' show. The stage is set. The audience is in its place. The actors - time of day, season, weather, direction, sea - deliver their lines. Voices speak from the sepulchre of the lost village. The ghosts of brave hearts lying asleep in the deep awake and join the chorus. What are they saying? The performance is inspirational. It is more than entertainment. It is a conspectus of image and reality, of classicism and pantomime, of time and space, of sound and light, of the sensual and the spiritual. The standing ovation continues all the way home. Encore. There's always tomorrow.

How Chichester has Learned

George Appleby

In the modern classic *How Buildings Learn* (Viking, 1994), Stewart Brand celebrates buildings that adapt to the changing needs of those who use them. He points out that from their first drawing, buildings are shaped and (the adaptable ones) reshaped by changing cultural currents, real estate values and usage. Of those that cannot adapt a few become museum pieces; all the others sooner or later get demolished.

Amongst the many buildings worldwide that Brand celebrates in point of adaptive success is St. Mary's Hospital, Chichester. Built in 1295 as a hostel for the homeless, with an integral chapel, it was converted to an almshouse in 1535 to provide 8 two-roomed dwellings for old people. Over the last hundred years or so it has been further altered to give residents better heating, lighting, insulation and ventilation as standards and technological resources improved. Thus we have, on our doorstep in Chichester, an 800-year-old building still with us, because it could respond to changing social needs and standards - which is why it still contributes its beautiful roof, to take the most obvious feature, to the city's townscape.

Had Brand not been drawing on an international array of buildings that learn, he might have noted several more in Chichester, a city that has responded more successfully than most to social, industrial and technological change. Consider today's use of the Market Cross, the city walls, town houses and their gardens, the Roman road that brought the town into

ST MARY'S HOSPITAL
Chichester

being, and the Cathedral. Almost as soon as it was built, this fortified staging post on the road system of an occupying power changed into a market town: a place of meeting, trade and exchange of information. Over the next millennia as the nature of the social and economic activities changed, the city changed with them.

Thus, the market cross, supplied by a canny Tudor bishop as a trade centre, became, when thickening traffic forced removal of the market from East Street, a meeting point for residents (especially the young) and city businesses, notably lawyers' clerks exchanging local mail. And when Chichester became a resort town in a holiday area, the Cross became, with restoration, a key tourist attraction.

Macdonald's must have, in East Street, one of their most imposing shop fronts and layouts. Prior to this, especially in the days before television, the building had been a flourishing cinema, but that splendid portico belongs to its original function as the central Corn Exchange for the area's farmers.

In point of adaptation, would demolition of the old Exchange and the erection of a purpose-built Macdonald's (much like those, say, in Worthing or Portsmouth) have been an improvement? Would it have been any more commercially successful?

To the rear of the Corn Exchange is a substantial building once divided into stores, shops and offices for farm-related activities; over the years the activities became steadily less farm-related and eventually the whole block was purchased by John Wiley and converted into a branch of their publishing business (winning a Pilgrim Trust award in the process.)

THE CORN EXCHANGE
Chichester

Sadler's Walk, which the writer first visited in the 1950s, had been a two-level store supplying horticulture and garden equipment (though not, as he had hoped, saddles and bridles). In the early 1990s it was rebuilt as a shopping arcade. Similar retail development in response to the needs of today's shopper, who views shopping as partly leisure activity, is evident in the 1980s conversion of the alms houses in the Hornet into a much smaller arcade - the Welfare State of the day having (apparently) made almshouses redundant.

There are other adaptations from the old farming industry: Bartholomew's Seeds (North Walls), now flats and a fitness studio; The Tannery (Westgate), now WSCC architect's offices; and, of course, the Cattle Market itself. Livestock was bought and sold at this market right up to the late 1980s. This space is now given over to car parking although its twice-weekly stalls market remains hugely popular with visitors as well as locals. The market's continuing presence is thanks to the fight put up by the Chichester Society to resist the erection of a multi-storey car park and supermarket on the site plus the building of a link road. Correspondingly, the stalls of the old Butter Market are still used though for far more than dairy produce. The area off the Hornet where needlemaking once went on became first barns for a seed merchant, then shops for gardening supplies and, after a less successful fight, a link road. However, the barns that survived were turned into flats.

Provision of entertainment goes hand-in-hand with any market town's economic function. The Marks & Spencer's branch which opened in North Street in this decade, replaced Perrings the carpet and furniture store; Perrings, some thirty years before, had taken over Kimbell's dance hall and restaurant which had been as good a place as any for making new acquaintances. Such a facility is much missed today, if not by the ageing population that protests at any suggestion of night club development, because of the noise it might generate, then certainly by younger people who have to go to an adapted farm building (Thursdays Club near Oving) or to Bognor, or else to the pubs.

The popularity of the movies in the 1930s produced, in addition to the Granada in Corn Exchange, the Odeon (South Street), the Gaumont (Eastgate Square), and the Electric Cinema (Northgate). As this medium lost popularity in the 1960s, the Electric became a storage barn (and has been ever since), the Odeon a supermarket (now Iceland), and the Gaumont a swimming bath. Chichester has always been slow, if not niggardly, in point of public provision, and much of the cost of the Gaumont's conversion was borne by fund-raising local citizens. (Compare the Festival Theatre, New Park Centre, Squash and Tennis Club.) When, at last, a purpose-built pool system was provided at Westgate, local people campaigned to have the old baths and cinema turned into a youth amenity, perhaps bowling alley or dance hall. But the council refused to respond, and, at the time of writing, are offering the area west of the East Walls for redevelopment. Any bets on how little this development will offer to the community, especially its young?

A whole book could be written about adaptations concerning alcohol provision. The sixteenth-century inns - *The Punchbowl*, and *The White Horse* - were originally substantial town houses; *The Victoria* pub in St. Pancras (originally a brewery), is now converted to offices and its bottling plant to the rear is the Metro restaurant. The pub and hotel trade as a whole might seem to be in recession at present to judge from the fate of *The Victoria* and *The Cattle Market Inn* (now occupied by Age Concern and a shoe repair shop), *The Fleece* in East Street which is now an estate agents and *The Dolphin and Anchor*, converted recently to Waterstone's, Edinburgh Woolshop and a restaurant. As a coaching inn the *Dolphin* had been the starting point for the first Chichester to London run. On the other hand there is the recently opened Smith & Western restaurant, adapted from the redundant railway goods building that had been essential when cattle and feedstuffs were being brought into market. A controversial adaptation is that of the former parish church of St Peter into a pub, *The Slurping Toad*, after a period as a 1980s shopping mall. Those who deprecate its closeness to the cathedral and its popularity with the young ignore the fact that in the early part of the century there were no fewer than eight pubs within shouting distance of the Close.

Adaptation of church buildings further illustrates the principle: adapt, survive and please. This century has seen some 90% decline in the churchgoing population. Has Chichester demolished redundant churches? Indeed not. In 1950 St Olave's (Chichester's oldest single-cell church) became the SPCK bookshop, and in 1960 the Bible Christian Chapel in the Hornet became a Chinese takeaway. The open-preaching style layout of St John's Chapel makes it popular for concerts (every day during the Chichester Festivities) and the massive cathedral itself is filled during that season with big name events (e.g. Humphrey Lyttleton and his band). The Bishop's Palace would have failed long ago had not much of it been taken over by the Prebendal School, which has grown in size since becoming coeducational.

George Appleby

BIBLE CHRISTIAN CHAPEL
Chichester

As the city flourished over the centuries many fine houses were built both within and without the walls, most of which have seen adaptation. One of the finest is the house called Murray's (after its owner) which became The Ship Hotel; its staircase is a model of eighteenth-century proportion and elegance. Nearly opposite is Fernleigh, also eighteenth century with flint-faced walls, its many rooms providing a variety of communitycentre resources on behalf of the County Council. Or consider Pallant House Art Gallery that had previously been used as offices and a council chamber by the District Council. In the eighteenth century it was the home of a prosperous ship owner who had a platform built on the roof from where, it is said, he could survey his ships in Chichester

Harbour. The list of such conversions, reincarnations and reinterpretations from private to public use and back again is very extensive. Many small residences, singly or collectively, became shops; most of the Georgian houses in the Pallants have become flats or offices or, for reasons of expense, both. The town house on the south side of Eastgate Square where John Keats wrote much of 'The Eve of St. Agnes' is currently a hairdressers and camping equipment shop.

Developments in educational provision further make the point: while the school for choir boys adapted in this century to meet more general educational needs, the Oliver Whitby School on the north side of West Street was put out of business by the 1944 Education Act and its classrooms were swallowed up by the city's most successful department store, then Morants, now Army & Navy.

On the other side of the city the Victorian school (built 1888) at New Park Road became redundant in the early 1960s when its pupils were moved out to modern coeducational premises at Orchard Street, which were bigger with better lighting, heating, catering and administrative facilities generally. The empty classrooms were then used by local groups. (e.g. Chichester Players, Chichester Judo Club). In 1975, because the building was old, uncared for and leaking, the Council proposed to demolish, but the clubs, supported by the Chichester Society, mounted a successful campaign to save it. Since then the New Park Centre has gone from strength to strength, recently becoming home to an Arts Cinema that shows four or five different films each week. The point about 'how buildings learn' is particularly relevant here: three high-ceilinged classrooms have been converted longitudinally into a mat-sports gymnasium, one classroom (horizontally) into theatre dressing rooms, with a scenery store above, and two other classrooms into a theatre/cinema where tiered seating can be folded away to provide space for a children's playgroup in the mornings.

New Park Centre is currently in danger because planners, wishing to sell off the decaying swimming bath/cinema site

George Appleby

NEW PARK CENTRE
Chichester

(see above), believe they have to offer to a potential developer the adjacent car park area plus the old school as well. The federation of clubs that run the Centre protest that they have worked hard over 25 years to make the place the success it has become. The Council reply that developers will be briefed to supply purpose-built replacements; but the federation argues that the building has a special quality because of what it has learned over the last quarter of a century in responding to the needs of different groups and to the energies of the people involved. Purpose-built facilities would be soulless and uninspiring of the volunteer effort that the old school generates. And they would not be loved.

As Brand argues, the disadvantage of today's structures is their steel and concrete inflexibility. Rapid technological change rapidly alters economic and social needs, but few of today's buildings can adapt as successfully as their predecessors. What the story of Chichester underlines is that the buildings that learn to meet new needs, not only do so more interestingly, but usually do it more cheaply and, in doing so, add to the distinctive character of their environment.

THIRTY-TWO

Eric James Mellon: *A Casualty of War (1945)*

Ever since Duke William in 1066, Sussex has been aware of invasion, and these burned-out buildings from 1945 are a vivid reminder of that awareness. At the time, the artist, Eric James Mellon, was Quartermaster at a camp in Sidley, Bexhill, organized by Henry Lawrence Reeves, sometime curate-in-charge at St James, Watford (where Mellon first met him), but on the occasion of the camp officiating at St Augustine's, South Croydon. The farm buildings were accidentally fired by British soldiers, but because of contemporary interest in recording the ravages of war (Mellon particularly remembers exhibitions in London showing work by John Piper and Eric Ravilious), the subject appealed to the young artist and he sketched this record. The date was early August 1945, about a week prior to VJ Day.

Publication of work by artists such as Piper and Ravilious that showed the effects of war occurred as early as 1942 in a series of volumes, *War Pictures by British Artists*, published by Oxford University Press; volume II in the series is especially apposite as the introduction was by J. B. Morton.

THIRTY-THREE

KIPLING'S WHEELTRACKS

Molly Mahood

On a Sussex road in 1902, the proud owner of a Locomobile is being driven northward to rendezvous with a friend when a carrier's cart blocks his way. The steam car can produce a blast like a fog horn. When the horse stops bolting, the cart disgorges two naval warrant officers, acquaintances of the motorist, who continue their journey with him. One of them, a ship's engineer, joyously takes over the controls, but progress is uncertain in a vehicle that cannot go ten miles without several breakdowns and replenishments of oil, petrol (to fire the boiler) and water. When the party does achieve a downhill run they are stopped by a policeman out of uniform (the enraged carrier has telegraphed ahead) for exceeding the 12 mph limit. Their response is to lure the constable into the car and drive off with him. On a ridge of the High Weald the car breaks down - irreparably it would seem - but a *deus ex machina* appears: the waiting friend being the god and the machine his petrol-driven vehicle which carries the party and their terrified captive northeastward, then down to the Hastings road to 'circle enormously amid green flats fringed by martello towers' and thence westwards on the north side of the Downs until, at dusk, the victim is tipped out among the beavers and zebras kept by 'Sir William Gardener' and the others continue into Horsham for a good dinner.

According to Kipling's prefatory poem to 'Steam Tactics' (of which this is the gist), we should be rolling on the ground, helpless with laughter at this Heavenly Lark. Today's readers

RUDYARD KIPLING (1899)
Philip Burne-Jones
PAINTED IN KIPLING'S STUDY AT ROTTINGDEAN

223

are more likely to cringe before a story, told with a deadly inner-ring knowingness, of Edwardian hearties proclaiming their mastery over machines that are always 'she', and at the same time putting a member of the lower orders in his place - the company of even lower creatures in the wild life park at Leonardslee. However, the real Kipling enthusiasts - Ruddites, we might call them, on the model of Kipling's own telling 'Janeites' - have never been troubled by the spectre of Kipling the Hooligan. They have spent happy hours trundling up and down the roads of West Sussex, working out from such teasingly probable names as 'Pigginfold' the exact topography of the story's first part, that dozen miles of misadventures which culminates in the Locomobile retiring 'from active life in a flood of tears' in St Leonard's Forest.

So what am I - who find the story embarrassing, if not quite as much the product of Auden's 'horrible old Kipling' as his more sober revenge stories - doing on the A26 a mile or two south of Uckfield in East Sussex, looking for Kipling's wheeltracks with all the care of the most devoted Ruddite? The answer is on the car seat beside me in the form of a volume of Kipling's letters of 1900-1910 and of jottings taken from the surviving transcript of his wife's diary (thank you, University of Sussex). Between them they furnish me with a most Kipling-like knowingness.

Kipling's love affair with the car, they reveal, became serious in 1900, when he and his wife house-hunted all over Sussex in a car which they rented, complete with driver, for three and a half guineas a week. It was reliable enough to carry them from Rottingdean to Arundel and back in ten hours, and Kipling's letters reverberate with the splendours of this novel mode of transport. Next year however he discovered its miseries, when he bought the Locomobile. A letter ending 'Yours locomobiliously' chronicles the shame Coughing Jane brought upon his head: on June 26, two friends he tried to impress on a flat road had to 'pump dolefully all the way home'; on June 29 and on (I believe) this very hillside where I have pulled in, she 'blew through her cylinders, leaked and lay down'. A man came from London and worked at repairs all the next day. Three days later, when the Burne-Jones aunt was being taken for a drive along Brighton front the Locomobile 'shut down her fire automatically' and had to crawl to the repair shop amid the jeers of the trippers (whose intrusions at Rottingdean had already convinced Kipling that he had to find a house in the Weald). Small wonder that he thought at this point of meeting the repair bills by a journalistic piece, 'say 5000 words - under caption 'Locoed'', nor that when this nucleus of 'Steam Tactics' turned, a year later, into a would-be comical story of revenge he was still trying to exorcize the violent irritability - he was even to call it hysteria - that all these breakdowns induced.

And not only irritability. If the story's first part originates in Coughing Jane's June 29 performance on the A26, when, to quote another letter 'she did everything vile that a motor could do', the reason was that this was the most traumatic of all those bad days. Carrie Kipling was not well, and the couple were going to Crowborough to find somewhere their children could stay while she took a rest cure. She reached home totally exhausted by their mishaps and soon afterwards developed clinical depression, so that guilt and family anxiety were added to Kipling's nexus of emotions. And dominating all was the sense of frustration. It was not only the Locomobile that he could not make go at this time. He had not been able to establish himself as a Sussex landowner; Bateman's, which he coveted, had been withdrawn from the market. Creatively too, 1901 was proving a thin year for him. A few days as guest of the Fleet on its manoeuvres in the Channel were to lead to the re-invention of Petty Officer Pyecroft and a run of Pyecroft stories, but Kipling must have known in his heart that Pyecroft, whose navy-talk exasperates the reader of 'Steam Tactics', was a bore by comparison with Mulvaney of Soldiers Three. An even bigger frustration was that hardly anyone was prepared to listen to Kipling's strident calls to England - 'a stuffy little place mentally, morally and physically', he told Rhodes - to rearm, expand and modernise. Coughing Jane's inertia came to stand for that of the nation. When Carrie recorded 'Motoring verses' in her diary for December, what Kipling actually sent to *The Times* on that day was his savage indictment of 'flannelled fools at the wicket'.

RUDYARD KIPLING IN HIS FIRST MOTORCAR,
a Locomobile 'Steamer'

So there was plenty to contribute to Kipling's near-frenzy on the Crowborough road on June 29, 1901. But sitting here today in my blessedly reliable hatchback, I am picking up no vibes; and in the last year of the century it does not do to loiter by the roadside. 'All right, darling?' asks a passing police patrolman. I wonder how he would take it if I called him 'Robert', as the bully-boys do their captive policeman in 'Steam Tactics'. Time to move on towards Ashdown Forest, which is patently what Kipling means by the 'barren waste' of the story, though he calls it St Leonard's Forest in celebration of one day in that summer when, having successfully reached Handcross and joined friends from Guildford for a picnic in

on a common traversed by a Roman road that can only be Stane Street. Villages where bees 'boomed in eighty-foot lindens that overhung grey Norman churches' prove harder to find. The Normans liked their churches on eminences, and the Great Storm felled many trees in this area. Fittleworth church is not Norman, but giant lime trees nearby make its churchyard a pleasant place in which to read a story which, to judge from its opening paragraph, is going to be about that discovery of the Sussex past which Kipling held to be the greatest pleasure of motoring.

But for all its topographical start, that is not what 'They' is about. Nor is it easy, without clumsiness, to say just what it is about. An oblique approach may help: looked at one way, this is a story about the Car as a benign power. Somewhere in this part of Sussex, the car in question freewheels down a sunken lane to land its owner in the garden of a beautiful Elizabethan house. He hears and catches glimpses of several children before the blind woman, whose house it is, welcomes him and requests him to drive the car through the garden to please the children. A month later he returns, the car having taken the road 'of her own volition' (as even end-of-the-century cars have a way of doing). This time the engine breaks down on the edge of the park. But instead of throwing the expected tantrum the storyteller spreads out a glittering array of tools in the hope of luring the children from their hiding places. Still they elude him; and though the blind woman reappears, their talk is interrupted by the news that a child on the estate is gravely ill. The car, now back in running order, enables its owner speedily to find a doctor who in turn commandeers him and his vehicle in order to fetch medicines from the county town and to scour the district for a nurse (found at last in 'a convent of French nuns' - presumably at West Grinstead). In spite of all these efforts the child dies, as the motorist discovers on a third visit. This time the blind woman takes him on a tour of the house which, like the garden, seems to have been made for children and is strewn with signs of their presence. But They continue to play their game of hide-and-seek with both the chatelaine and her guest; it is only while he is sitting in the shadows listening to her deal capably with a difficult tenant, that he at last feels his hand taken and there is planted upon it 'the little brushing kiss' which is 'a fragment of the mute code devised very long ago. Then I knew.'

Is it that the blind woman's fantasies about the children she has not been able to bear have summoned into tangible life the daughter whom the narrator has lost? Or has his grief and that of others - among them the butler, and the mother of the child who has died in the course of the story - fed her longing by giving audible life to her dream children? Such questions, raised by the delicate, Jamesian ambiguity of the story, hang unresolved above the graves in the lime-scented air, and then, as its spell fades, give place to a more direct and simple question: what house hereabouts, between Horsham and the scarp of the Downs, inspired Kipling to write 'They'?

I return to my driving seat and an answer jumps at me off the local OS map, Parham! I can even put my thumbnail on a closely contoured lane from the south which could have carried Kipling straight down to the 'ancient house of lichened and weatherworn stone' backed by 'marshalled woods'. But for today's Very Many People the approach is from the north. Twenty minutes later my Micra has added its gleam to the lake of parked cars. And as I peep into the Victorian nursery, note the good hiding places on the stairs and scope for races in the gallery, and wish I were small enough to enter the rooms built into the garden wall, I remember that this house, that indeed seems made for children, was owned, when Kipling was exploring Sussex, by a childless couple. I go in quest of information - and come away crestfallen. There is no record of Kipling ever having visited Parham. As for the miniature house-in-the-wall, it was built in 1928.

So back to Kipling's description; and now I begin to see Parham will not do. The house in the story is red-roofed, not Horsham-tiled as are big houses in this part. Slim brick chimneys, a dovecote, clipped yews . . . what does all that remind me of . . . Why, Bateman's! Yet surely Kipling's story starts *from* Bateman's? His traveller has driven from 'the orchid-studded flats of the East', across the Downs, along the coast and into the Low Weald near Chanctonbury Ring - But now, suddenly, I realise that the brilliance of Kipling's evocation of this particular bit of Sussex has tricked me into the Ruddite literalism I laughed at. The lane leading to the house is so authentic a Sussex sunken road, exactly matching the one that earlier I followed down, down, down from Bedham to Fittleworth, that only now, returning to the story's opening, do I realise the route taken by the motorist is the dreamer's traditional descent into another kingdom, another state of being. If 'They' can be said to start from any literal place, it is from a house six thousand miles away from Sussex,

'BATEMAN'S'
W. Monk, R.E.
Rudyard Kipling's house at Burwash

on the slopes of Table Mountain. There, in the hot grape-harvest days of 1904, Kipling, it would appear, at last came to terms with the worst thing to have happened to him.

In their long house-hunt at the beginning of the century, Kipling and his wife were not just fleeing Brighton sightseers. They were running away from a haunted house. Rottingdean became intolerable for them after the death of their six-year-old daughter Josephine, which had occurred on a visit to New York early in 1899. When their motoring began in 1900, every drive into a countryside rich in the relics of a past that was not their past was a day's escape: every house they looked at on those drives offered them, potentially, an escape for good. Though the most desirable one slipped through their fingers at first, they moved into it late in 1902 and when Kipling wrote his story about a house which combines, in the manner of dreams, features of the houses he had viewed the length and breadth of Sussex with the one he finally lived in, he had passed a whole spring, summer and autumn - the seasons of the three drives in the story - at Bateman's.

Meanwhile the bereavement syndrome took its natural course, as the pain of remembering gave way to unease at the failure to persist in remembrance. 'I have never seen the faces of my dead in any dream' the narrator of 'They' tells the blind woman, Readers who find 'They' sentimental focus on the moment of conjuration, on the kiss, and if the story ended there their misgivings would be justified. But the woman and her guest continue to talk. She excuses herself for keeping the fire in all night; it is so that They may always find warmth. At this, the narrator tells us, he looked at the hearth and saw, 'through tears I believe, that there was no unpassable iron near it'. Here I believe is the nub of the tale. The children of the childless do not need a fireguard; only those who have borne - the verb serves subtly to encompass the other parent - know what it is to live with anxiety and that grief for the dead cannot be indulged at the cost of our vigilance for the living.

For the traveller, as for Kim at his parting from the Lama, a choice has to be made, only here it is not represented by 'separate sides of my head' but by houses, one real and one envisioned, on separate sides of the county. He decides never to return. 'For you it is right . . . for me it would be wrong'. By 1904, Kipling had an unhaunted hearth of his own on which to maintain the sacred flame that is a motif of the tale. He had two younger children to protect, to live for - and to write for. The achievement of 'They' is not in its power as a ghost story, but in its evidence that Kipling reached the calm of mind he was feeling his way towards when, in a letter of condolence written late in 1900, he wished his correspondent 'such comfort as men say time brings after loss. It's apt to be a weary while coming but one goes the right way to get it if one interests oneself in the happiness of other folk even though the sight of that happiness is like a knife turning in a wound'. This tune goes manly; we are a world away from the petulant, aggressive *machismo* of much of Kipling's writing of the Boer War years.

'They' is not an unflawed story. The author of 'Steam Tactics' cannot stop being a know-all (here, about masonic symbolism, of all things) and cannot wholly suppress a jarring class-consciousness. But these blemishes do not keep the story from taking its place in a great elegaic tradition that reaches back to Tennyson's 'touch of a vanished hand' and forward, by Eliot's own admission, to the dream children of Burnt Norton - 'Hidden excitedly, containing laughter'. As I take my own way back eastwards at the foot of the Downs, on the single-track underhill road that in the dusk is as unfrequented as the lanes Kipling travelled, I reflect that, just as we endure traffic jams, road rage and near-misses in the faith that the car will sometimes afford us deep pleasures of liberation and discovery, I can tolerate Kipling at his most impossible in the knowledge that, at his best, he can deliver a story such as 'They'.

THIRTY-FOUR

ON CHITHURST BRIDGE

Chris Sparkes

It was a bright evening in the beginning
of May, and we leaned on the stone bridge
that double-arches over the slow River Rother

where, as a small boy, forty years ago,
I used to fish for trout with the dull ratchet
of an old wooden reel.

The swifts had arrived early
and were doing their aerial dirt-tracking
around the yew tree in the graveyard

of the thousand year old chapel
sinking there in high grass. They screamed
through white hot draughts of wind,

flitted and sailplaned in scribbled loops,
zooming past the bell-tower,
then cooled their wings off

high above the chapel roof. Upstream
the river bends away, and is covered over
by hanging branches, so sight of it

is lost. But suddenly through those low alders
we saw a disc of light,
a long way up-river

between the emerald leaves,
where faster moving water was caught in sunlight,
and it shimmered like tin-foil

through that small space,
as if some huge afternoon star
had fallen into trees.

THIRTY-FIVE

Joy Whiting: CHAPEL SPIRE AT UNIVERSITY COLLEGE CHICHESTER

The chapel, built in the early 1960s, was designed by Peter Shepheard; on the exterior there is a Geoffrey Clarke sculpture (a large tree-like form, holding a nugget of glass - the eye of God), and inside hangs *Creation*, a fine tapestry by Jean Lurçat.

Joy Whiting: OPPORTUNISTS AT COLWORTH, NEAR CHICHESTER

WHEELBARROW FARM, CHARLTON - now derelict (left)

CRICKET AT THE CASTLE:
AN ARUNDEL EXPERIENCE

Michael Marshall

The cricket ground at Arundel Castle was carved out of a slope in The Downs in 1895. The work was carried out by Estate workers who otherwise would have been unemployed during the agricultural recession of that time.

This was one of the many building projects in which Henry, 15th Duke of Norfolk concerned himself. A widower for over ten years, and the father of a seriously disabled only son who was soon to die, he assuaged personal grief through his vast range of public activities. In addition to his responsibilities as Earl Marshal and as the Catholics' principal layman, he used his family's considerable fortune, acquired through land interests in many parts of the country, for a wide range of building projects. At Arundel, this was reflected not only in the restoration work on the Castle, but in the construction of the nearby Catholic Cathedral - vast in size for so small a town. When it came to the construction of a cricket ground, Duke Henry enquired which was the largest playing surface in England. On hearing that it was the Kennington Oval, he said 'Make mine bigger'.

The Duke was already too old to perform as a cricketer and the cricket played on his ground in the early days provided recreation for the Estate workers and those employed on rebuilding the Castle. For outside opposition, they relied on local teams of which the first recorded example was in a game against the West Sussex Gazette in 1897 (whose team described themselves as 'The Scribblers').

It was only with the Duke's second marriage to Gwendolen Constable-Maxwell, or Duchess Gwendy as she was affectionately known, that country house cricket began at Arundel. Through her vast array of Scottish and Yorkshire relations, house parties were organized to play against each other as well as the local town side, Army teams drawn from those on annual military manoeuvres in the Park and in the start of a series of matches against the Fitzroy Somerset family from Goring Castle

Cricket on a more sustained basis followed with the coming of age in 1929 of Duke Henry and Duchess Gwendy's son, Duke Bernard (who had succeeded to the title on his father's death in 1917). It was he who was responsible for the first serious effort to both develop the ground and to increase its cricket activities.

To the great maple and chestnut trees and the oak planted by Queen Victoria during her visit to Arundel in the last century, Duke Bernard added other trees, shrubs and plants so that the ground was virtually encircled. His particular inspiration, however, was to create a wide gap in the trees revealing a great fold of The Downs and the Arun River valley as it stretches away to the north. It is this view, together with the abundant wildlife and glimpses of the Castle and the Cathedral which make many declare this the most beautiful cricket ground in the world.

But the heritage which we enjoy today is not just - in the official jargon - an Area of Outstanding Natural Beauty. It is also the true home of cricket, the last bastion of how the game should be played and a training ground in which these values may be encouraged and sustained from the earliest age. Part of this process - most notably the cricket school built behind the pavilion in recent years is the work of Duke Bernard's successors. But the spirit of sportsmanship, the sense of fun and the fellowship of cricket were all values, which were directly inculcated by the 16th Duke in matches he organized

THE CRICKET GROUND
at Arundel Castle

between 1930 and 1974. In doing so, he created a unique blend between country house cricket and the game at near First Class level which opened the way to visits by leading Club, County and Test Touring Sides.

Yet all these visitors and the regulars chosen for the home side were soon made aware of what some have described as, 'The Laws of cricket as decreed by Bernard, Duke of Norfolk'. These laws bear little resemblance to the laws propounded by the MCC. For example, the injunction 'The side winning the toss shall ensure that his Grace's side bats last' was, and is, intended to ensure that the privilege of chasing a winning total is normally reserved for the host's team.

Those who failed to recognize this local custom paid a heavy price. One well-known Club, side which came to Arundel as part of its centenary celebration, won the toss, put the Duke's team in to bat on a green wicket and dismissed them for a low score. The match ended in a defeat for the home team in the early afternoon. It should be noted that, in the almost four decades since, there has been no return match. Equally, the Duke's aversion to safety first cricket is still respected. Near the end of his life when he had given up appearing on the field, he would sit in a great chair at the top of the steps in front of the pavilion and direct operations. One young Sussex 2nd XI player discovered that ducal advice superseded his Captain's instructions. On going out to bat for the Duke, he suggested, following the sudden fall of several wickets, 'Perhaps its time to put up the shutters'. Before his Captain could reply, a booming voice from the
top of the steps rang out 'Not if you hope to play on this ground again, you won't'.

There was, too, the matter of punctuality. Duke Bernard's early Army career and his work in organising great State occasions had all given him the strictest interpretation of time keeping. When players arrived on his ground late with the familiar excuse of traffic delays, they would be greeted by the Duke's steely-eyed look and the remark, 'What you really mean is that you left too late to be here on time'.

The recognition of these values and the occasional interposing of local rules has been sustained to this day by a dedicated team determined to maintain cricket at the Castle in the Duke's memory. They have done so at a time when it seemed that massively increased commercialisation of the game and its corollary of winning at all costs were affecting all levels of the game.

Through the personal generosity of Duke Bernard's widow, Duchess Lavinia and his daughters, together with the formation of a fee-paying Arundel Castle Cricket Club membership, other outside sponsorship and the recruitment of skilled administrators, the Ground was host this year to over 50 matches and cricket events. These range from school and youth cricket competitions for Under I Is, Under 16s and an England v. Australia Under 19s Test Match, to the provision of a home ground for the Sussex Martlets, two Sussex County games against Leicestershire and Middlesex and the traditional touring team match involving, this year, the New Zealand World Cup team. In addition, provision was made for 15 matches for the Earl of Arundel's team to take on, among others, Oxford, Cambridge, Combined Services, MCC, Australian Crusaders, South African Cavaliers and the traditionally hard-fought Local Derby against the Arundel town side as well as the more exotic challenge from the Actors of the Chichester Festival Theatre.

The success in building up this fixture list results from long-standing connections with the MCC and the Sussex County Cricket Club. When Duchess Lavinia founded her Club, she was fortunate in attracting the support of Billy Griffith, formerly of Sussex and England and a long-serving Secretary of the MCC. He in turn brought in Ronnie Ford, former Assistant Secretary of MCC. Between them, they built up the cosmopolitan fixture list and ensured that, despite modern money demands, international touring teams continue the now long standing tradition of playing one of their opening matches at Arundel.

Today, the future of the Club seems assured through the

THIRTY-SEVEN

ON THE ROAD TO ARRAS

Patrick Garland

It had been a year of discontent, and petty irritation. Nothing disastrous on the grand scale, but a sequence of uneventful setbacks. His bachelor-life was happy enough, but it seemed to oppress him lately in a way it hadn't before. There had been too much rain; he had witnessed a dog run over in front of him while he waited for a bus. His job at the South East Poets had begun to seem unimportant, even boring, which he had not experienced before. There were minor affairs connected with money, some hoped-for projects had not come off. He no longer enjoyed music, and he disliked intensely every new play he had seen. The doctor said his mental state was far from a nervous collapse, but there was an unidentified crisis of sorts.

He had not enjoyed a holiday for three years, nor had he known the luxury of being by himself. His superior was sympathetic, and so it was mutually agreed he should go away by himself at Easter, and enjoy a short walking tour in Northern France. He had never been there, had always wanted to go. His doctor agreed what he needed was a short uneventful holiday. Before the Easter holidays began, he packed a suitcase and prepared to quit Hove. He thought he might find an opportunity to re-read Edmund Gosse's *Father and Son,* and slipped it into his pocket; it would amuse him, and pass the time.

Christopher Casdagli had this little job at the South East Poets, and worked in a comfortable office overlooking

Brunswick Square. His enemies called it 'Poet's Corner'.

He had always liked the town, had been brought up there as a child, and even now felt reassured by its affluent Squares, and their patches of tidy parkland along the sea-front. He relished the apparent seediness of the backstreets and bric-à-brac shops.

His work at the South East Poets involved committees mainly, and he was 'capable' on these occasions. It was absurd, simply because he was both taciturn and lacking in ambition to assume that he was dull. Neither his friends, nor his colleagues, found him so, and the poets he met from time to time respected him, even cared about him.

Poetry, unlikely though it was, was his profession. He had the responsibility, as Secretary to a regional literary panel, of selecting likely candidates for government grants, sometimes individuals, sometimes groups, and even literary societies. Once he had enjoyed the satisfaction of recommending (and obtaining) the sum of Five pounds, fifty pence, towards the Blake Society of Felpham, an enterprising little group from West Sussex. But he himself had never been, nor indeed wanted to be, a poet. In fact, he rather disliked poets, found them to be generally egoistic, and constantly vain. Not that he bothered about egoism or vanity in other people, but in poets he would have preferred something more dignified. He seldom found it. Frequently the poets of his experience grumbled, sometimes they grovelled. A friend of his referred to 'a whinge of writers'. Whenever he met poets socially they never talked of anything except money. He preferred the company of some of his colleagues in the publishing, or the university world. He thought bureaucrats, in his experience, more noble. Of course, Casdagli admitted the idea of academe, and donnish life, but not for himself. He valued the external façade of quietness, but knew from experience that behind the porticoes and walnuts, the quadrangles seethed with intrigue, suspicion, jealousy, and even dislike. Inward silence there was not, and he valued the quiet life. Besides he was no trencherman. So, he returned happily to his office on the third floor, with its curious view of bus-lanes, conveniences and grey sea, and typed memos concerning small bequests, and applications from impoverished poets all over the country. He collected shrewdly, and wrote down occasional remarks overheard among the literati which he thought merited preservation. This was an enterprise which occasionally proved satisfactory. 'Library graffiti', he smiled inwardly. The critic, Henrickson, an embittered man, had doodled one afternoon, 'I think this wretched poet looks for more hands to feed him, in order that he may have more hands to bite'. Another time he came across an empty pad, and the one word on it . . . 'loneliness'. It summed up a great deal of his own feeling at that moment, as well as whoever wrote it. His work could be depressing. So many of the poets he knew were in distress. Economic, or emotional distress, anguish from lack of recognition, unable to cope with their wives, incapable of paying their bills, and then, without warning, killing themselves. Casdagli frequently wondered, during these outbursts of despair he had to listen to, whether the whole business was worth it. Few of the poets were much good, and even fewer were contented. Some were neither good nor contented. Largely unpublished, constantly underpaid, cadging drinks, picking up tips underneath tea cups left for the waitress, dressed in awkward clothes, with none of the ease of a well-dressed man, and none of the confidence of a badly dressed one either. However, there were some poets he made exception of, and welcomed their very rare visits. This happy few always lived in the country, and frequently far away, in remote corners of the country at that. He had got on extremely well with Siegfried Sassoon, and managed to see the great survivor once a year, until his death. Once, the poetry panel decided they should honour Sassoon over his eightieth birthday. Casdagli, as an acquaintance, was elected to write, asking what kind of celebration, or honour, the poet would wish for. He was overjoyed to receive, by return of post, in the poet's cramped, but careful hand, the following message:

'The kindest honour I could wish for my eightieth birthday, is that it be passed over with the same discreet silence, as was my seventieth.'

His final day at the Brunswick Square office demanded of him a particularly unpleasant decision. He was required to select, from over four hundred entries, the final list of applicants for five substantial government bursaries. The decision bothered him, because it was both purposeless, and deeply serious at the same time. Had he been a socialist town-councillor, the decision would have been simple in the extreme. He would give the greater part of the money to whomever was judged to be the poorest. But the poetic world was more complicated than the socialist one. He knew, for example, that the most needful poet was not necessarily the best, and the best poet was not necessarily the one who would put the money to the most responsible use. And, whoever got it, it was extremely arguable that the bursary would produce better poetry. Someone on the Committee (a woman whom Casdagli particularly disliked) had suggested that benevolent literary panels had no business to take away poverty, pain, and wretchedness from a poet in the first place. An unpopular point of view, with which Casdagli privately inclined to sympathize. As always, he found himself enraged beyond measure at the inadequacy of the biographical material each sponsor was required to give to support their candidate. Some gave barely no information at all; others gave a great deal too much. The indifferent ones indolently wrote out a list of published works; others went into complex personal details. Among the fat folder of applicants, Casdagli picked out a handful that appeared discerning. A schoolboy of high promise here, a hospice matron of neglected abilities there, but the most part were fakes, over-pretentious, mental cases, or perfectly straightforward human beings with no talent whatsoever, who should be married, live in suburbs, and work in railway ticket-offices; people like himself, Casdagli thought bitterly. Was he bitter, he wondered? Conceivably. Hard to tell. Had he wanted to be a famous writer? Yes, but then, most people do. Did he want to write now? Yes. Had he the time, the occasion? Yes. Had he the ability? Questionable. Did he count writers among his friends? Never.

He put the plastic folder of applicants into a tray, making at the end a hurried, almost improvised decision, which seemed to him possibly correct. He placed on top of the file the application of a greengrocer, who longed to give up greengrocering, and placed beneath it, the request of a single woman who lived in Millom, a beastly little town on the coast of Cumbria. He had had the misfortune to be posted there during his war services, and felt sympathetic to anybody in so perilous a situation. He left his desk tidied, said goodbye to his immediate superior, a harassed man with an ulcer, and a white patch in his hair like a badger, and took the train first to Victoria, and - changing at Embankment, District and Northern Line, - to Waterloo. How he used to enjoy the old night-train and go to sleep in Waterloo Station, and wake up the next morning in Normandy. He would take his *petit dejeuner* early, and watch from the window of the dining-car, farmers out shooting, walking home with shotguns under their arms.

Nowadays it was three boring hours on Eurostar, time for a cup of coffee and a brisk read of a morning paper - but it always made him feel good to be back in France. Sometimes he wished to have been born French, or to have become French by marrying a Frenchwoman, but the only Frenchwoman he ever seriously loved had turned his proposal down. He changed his trains with the satisfaction of experience, gratified by his perfect recall of 'restaurant French'. He left the train at Amiens.

It had been his intention, and his doctor's, that he should explore the former battlefields of the Old Front Line. It was not as gruesome as it appears, for this was a pilgrimage he had always wanted to make. His father had survived the war to end all wars, but nevertheless had fought along those squalid trench-lines, and (dead for some years) left Casdagli with a vivid memory of raiding parties, of calm behaviour under fire, the courage of officers, the doggedness of private soldiers. He had read and enjoyed the war-poets, possibly more than any other kind of poetry; he had shared their disillusion, without having to experience it. He admired their sensitivity, and wondered, as had all their critics, what poetry they might have written had they returned home. And what people they might have become. What careers? Rupert Brooke, he realized, would have turned into a socialist politician; Wilfred Owen into holy orders, perhaps; and his friend, Siegfried, retired, quietly growing roses in a West Country garden, with that devastating barrage exploding inside his head.

He took a series of country autocars through Alaincourt, Barly, Albert, Berneville, plain villages most of them, until he found the signposts to Beaucourt and Arras. Curious, thought Casdagli, from his safe seat in the autocar, the unimaginative repetitions of history. How many invading armies, or retreating ones, had slogged along these dull flat fields, from Harfleur to Agincourt, the road to Arras, the withdrawal to Dunkirk. Struck by the irony, he took out a note-book and attempted to make some sort of a poem out of it. But it didn't work out. The landscape outside was so tedious he fell asleep.

He woke up when the bus stopped at a place called Dainville, and got out. He was the only one. No other English visitors, thank heaven.

It was Easter Sunday. Casdagli found himself a decent, small hotel, rather delightfully situated on a tributary of the river. He avoided conversation with the *patronne*, whom to his dismay he saw speaking aloud with her fat, grey cat. His room overlooked the water, and faced a modernised house-boat on the opposite bank, with television aerial, and washing on a line. Opening his window, he leant outside on his elbows, hearing the sounds of a raucous comedy programme in French floating across the water.

He ate dinner by himself, a muddy fish, unwisely recommended by the patronne, and drank a full carafe of red wine. His recipe for contentment was to go to bed slightly

the trees over there. Do you see that beech out in front, split in two? That's where it landed. Not eight feet away. We were on a practice shoot, what's more, in the forward O.P. It would be my good luck to get mine on a practice turn-out.'

'God, I hope not!'

'There's nowhere to go at the rear, in any case. Nothing to do. Nothing decent to eat. I usually stay in my billet and play the gramophone. Same old records. Re-read all my old letters. Write new ones.'

'Married?'

'Wife. Three children. One of them's a baby, really. They live in Essex now. Bloody awful ugly house. Used to live in a lovely cottage on the Downs, in a place just like this. I suppose in way that's why I like it here. I enjoy a lot of things out here, I used to enjoy at home. Perhaps that's the best way.'

The two men sat together in silence. The quietness of the woods enveloped them.

Casdagli, who was thirty-eight the previous June, suspected he must be about the same age as the seige Gunner next to him. They were both in their late thirties, and yet he knew for a certainty that almost eighty years separated them. He did not try to understand - everything was so ordinary, so unforced, so commonplace - why he should be seated next to a soldier and poet who had been killed in action in April 1917. 'I'll tell you something,' said Thomas, interrupting the quietness, but talking for all that in a low, almost confidential voice; 'this place one of these days is going to be the hottest corner this side of hell. If it is this side. I don't know why the Huns don't counter-attack Arras. Look all round you. Beyond this little copse, just a flat straight crest with trees. This could be any corner of Sussex flatland - the same kind of peaceful scrub, lacking alone the scoop of white chalk on the rough ground. And under the surface, think of it, below the turf, hundreds of thousands of hidden troops in trenches, armed, grudging, uncomfortable, tormented. But from eye-level, a silent, desolate scene without inhabitants. French pastoral, middle-nineteenth century. Minor Courbet, or even Corot.'

The soldier grappled in his pocket and pulled out a small notebook. It was bound in pigskin, and curiously creased and worn.

'Here it is', he said, and muttered something to himself, and closed 'The Notebook' again. Before he replaced it in his pocket, though, Casdagli interrupted him: 'Do you write things down then? Odd things that catch your eye?'

'It's a bit pointless really,' said Thomas, 'but when I was up here the other night, they were banging Dainville very heavily, and "the old Hun", as the Colonel calls him, gave these trees a regular shelling in the dark. I was sitting just where you are now, and all of a sudden the larks began singing. In the dark. Hell and perdition. Battle flaring all round. Larks. So I wrote down this.'

Thomas bent forward eagerly and showed him what looked like a new page of his notebook: Casdagli read the narrow handwriting:

> Where any turn may lead to heaven
> Or any corner may hide Hell.

'I suppose I might be able to make something of it,' he said. 'I write sometimes, when I get the opportunity. When I'm not too tired, and when I've finished censoring the chaps' letters.'

'Poetry?'

'Ideas for poetry, mostly. Notions, Images. They don't exactly flow, but sometimes I put bits and pieces together, you know'. He stopped short, and put 'The Notebook' away. 'The Colonel disapproves. Asked me once, as I was a writer, to write a letter to the local Mayor. Something about latrines.' His pipe had gone out, and he re-lit it, shielding his match from a slight breeze which stirred. Casdagli wrapped his coat about him.

Thomas hummed a few bars of ragtime to himself. 'Here, try a Cox's Pippin from Petworth Park.' And he pulled out a pair of apples from his voluminous pockets. 'Have you ever visited Arras?' he asked suddenly, biting into the rind.

'No', said Casdagli, 'I have never found the opportunity.'

'I went there in February with Thorburn and Lushington from

the Battery. It was uncanny. There'd been a raid, and the town was abandoned, but it was intact. That is, apart from one or two stray shells that had caught it, almost by accident, or so it looked. There was the small white square, quite empty. The Mairie. The little R.C. Church. And there was this house, and on the top floor, where a shell had ripped off the roof, this furnished room, like a scene out of a drawing room comedy when the curtain goes up, quite empty, but waiting for some actors to come in and liven the place up. Plus armchair, a table with a tablecloth still laid, an engraving hanging on the wall without its glass broken. I even read the date. 1850. And everything else impeccable, just at it ought to be. Farmhouse clock with a double chime. A dead man under a railway bridge. A grey calf, lying dead in a stable. And then, what I thought must have been a piece of black burnt paper, turned out to be a household bat. Just lying in the centre of the street. No sound at all.' He paused, and looked anxiously into the wood for a half second, the way a cat does when it spots a bird in the dense branches.

'False alarm,' he smiled, and relaxed. 'Still, I can't understand why the old Hun doesn't get started on Arras. If he's as fed up with sitting on his backside as I am, we might get this business finished with.' Thomas stood up, put his helmet back on, and patted Casdagli on the shoulder.
'Better be getting back to the Battery', he said; 'Debenham's getting pretty fed up with censoring their letters, although I rather enjoy it. My training as an anthologist helps me out. For all its faults a lot of their stuff is a great deal better than *The Countryman's Book of Verse*, let me tell you. Good luck, anyway.'
'What are you going to do next, Thomas?' Casdagli asked, as the officer started to walk away.
'When all this is over? Enjoy my work, mainly, I should think. Write, if I don't lose the trick of it. I don't think politics would do, and I'm not much good at anything else. I don't suppose I'll sign on, if that's what you're hoping.' Thomas turned hard on his heel, squatted down again, staring intensely. 'And - go

for good long walks . . . I know, I sound like the regimental quack, but I mean it. Look here, if you're with the Royal Sussex, you must know a little place called Flansham?'

Casdagli frowned in ignorance.

'It's a tiny little place with a handful of cottages and half a pub', near Blake's Felpham, if that rings a bell.'

'Just outside what the old queen used to call "dear little Bognor?"'

'That's the place. It's a dead-end village, really. Goes nowhere. When I lived at Berryfield, my walking companion, James Guthrie, he's a bit of a poet himself - looks like a Bishop - would meet me at Chichester Cross, and we'd tramp over to Flansham, through the barley and rye. Seven miles or so, and back again for hot mugs of tea at The Ship and Lighter. My last Thursday before enlisting, I remember I walked over the Downs to Flansham, swam in a rough cold sea, sat around the fire with Guthrie's youngsters singing songs, and back again under the stars . . .'

Casdagli could see from the officer's passionate stare and tense jaw, he was experiencing the rapture of that evening all over again.

'"Over the hills and far away", and a crescent moon. Guthrie with his dear old mouth-organ. One of the boys drumming the tambourine. Grand! And the long, exhilarating walk back home over the rough, unending Downs - the shadow of a ruined windmill in the wind.'

The eager siege-gunner folded both hands tightly around his pipe and puffed reflectively.

'Some days, you know, I feel as if I'm full of poems,' he said, 'and all I'd like is a little time to get them down.'

His smile fell sharply away, as a crack over the trees to the West signified the beginning of a sustained barrage.

'There it goes. Thought it wouldn't be long. In the direction of the old Chateau. It's a wonder there's anything left, they banged away at it last night. 600 rounds blind - in sleeting snow. The town's catching it badly these days. Go down there, past the mill, will you, there's some shelter there. This is only the prelude, I can tell you that. You infantry chaps don't know what it's like.' Thomas put his hand out, almost formally, as if they had been meeting at a luncheon party. 'We probably may not get together, so good luck again.'

'I suppose not.'

'Changing lines at the front, and all that.'

The noise of shrieking explosions grew louder now, and the wood echoed them, increasing their venom.

'Let's meet up here, if you get another chance. I'd like to talk to you about poetry, and the South Downs Way - I've walked it a time or two. The chaps at the battery don't usually go in for that sort of thing, but I enjoy it.' And suddenly, above the barrage, remembering the previous question, almost by way of an afterthought . . . 'Yes, write more poetry I should think. I'd like to be a poet, just as I'd like to live, but as I know as much about my chances in either case, I don't really care about either. Hello, we've gone out.' He put down his thornstick and, after groping for his matches, found them, and bent his head, clay pipe clenched, towards his cupped hands with the match.

There was the piercing whistle of a shell, and centimetres above his head Lieutenant Thomas fell gently forward onto his face. The body was unmarked, quite peaceful, as if sleeping, under its trenchcoat.

At the same time Casdagli felt the sky around him burst and break with the noise, trees uprooted themselves, somersaulted and split apart. Earth vomited in vast explosions, it stank like excrement. For a few moments the sky turned suddenly dark, vile yellow, the air in his lungs filled with poisonous sweet powder. Dense smoke tasted of blood and dung and cordite.

And then, the air lightened, and quite swiftly the noise disappeared. Casdagli was alone in the wood.

There was the ruined mill, and beside it, the drained pool. The trampled-down wire-fence, and the tidy plantation of conifers sloped up on each side in front of him. Three horsemen trotted slowly along a footpath, the horses' legs steaming a little, speckled with mud. One of the riders, a young woman in jeans and a Norwegian pullover, waved. They disappeared again into the wood. Casdagli sat there in silence, panting, and let silence overwhelm him. He heard the frantic pulse of his blood. And then, the hooves, invisibly squelching mud, moisture oozing out of the leaves. And from far away, unmistakably, the plaintive singing of larks.

Note:
Lieutenant Edward Thomas, G.S.A., was killed on the morning of April 9th, at 7.30 on the first day of the Battle of Arras, the beginning of the Spring Offensive. James Guthrie, the printer and craftsman, lived at South Harting and Flansham, and was E.T.'s frequent companion of long energetic walks across the South Downs, when the poet lived just on the Sussex-Hampshire border at Steep.

THIRTY-NINE

ALL OUR YESTERDAYS

Christopher Smith

Ask for me tomorrow, and you shall find me a grave man
(Shakespeare, *Romeo and Juliet*).

Years ago as a young and naive research student I spent three weeks in a Sheffield cemetery collecting data about Yorkshire's long departed daughters and sons. This may or may not sound like everyone's cup of tea, but my task was a very specific one: to assemble material on age of individuals at death in one corner of nineteenth-century England and, so armed, effect certain statistical manipulations of already-assembled census statistics - which would, in turn, permit estimates of actual birth rates amongst our ancestors a century ago. To say this sounds dry is akin to noting that Dickens was a competent novelist: the subject is mysterious, enthralling, and capable of changing how we think about the past.

To begin, it is necessary to scour mortality registers, rifling through thousands of cases: infants, children, adolescents, young adults, even a few older people. Deaths by accident occasionally, but in the main deaths by fever, deaths by ague, deaths by cholera, deaths by consumption, deaths by typhus, deaths overwhelmingly from nasty infectious agents that, in our sterile late twentieth-century bubble, it is easy to regard as unfamiliar. I suppose I learned intuitively that our ancestors dealt better with death than we do, for to them it was a much more familiar part of everyday life, and not something to shy away from like a squashed hedgehog in the gutter.

My work provided modest supporting evidence for a demographic transition in our society's recent past. The exercise was intrinsically technical and the sort of activity to keep an introvert content for an aeon: data was processed by computer, files manipulated and cross-tabulated, inferences drawn and noted. Yet in undertaking (oh dear!) this work, the analysis revealed how declining fertility was influenced by class, age, location, employment and, above all, by differential mortality. For if most poor young children died in infancy of something virulent and unpleasant, it was surely not unreasonable for their impoverished parents to produce many such offspring to guarantee the survival of a select few. Put like that, it may sound obvious, even trite, but truth is often simple and straightforward, even if hard to prove conclusively.

Armed with the knowledge and status that the analysis brought (for the work had led to a successful doctoral thesis), I then began to teach what I had learned.

This jump, from research student to lecturer, is not an easy one for it embraces the movement from introverted seeker after truth (whatever that is) to someone employed to perform in public. I knew my place, but I also recognized instinctively that the best lecturers are like the best actors: not brash extroverts relying on bluster, but well-prepared introverts employing a camouflage of apparent ease and spontaneity to mask a carefully-crafted professionalism. Perhaps insecurity and fear of failure are often the best nurturers of achievement and success ?

Yet, there was a real problem of presentation: how does one teach a subject as dehydrated as demography and win converts to my chosen area of expertise? And how does one do this in a systematic and consistent way ? In other words, how does one present a potentially alienating topic as so alive and vital that students would be keen to come back for more, and in turn spread the word that an understanding of demography was as exciting (and revealing) as the latest fashion garment from Milan or Paris.

So I invented a field exercise. I took some students to North Wales and deposited them in a cemetery. I told them to collect data. I told them what data to collect. Naturally, I had sought permission from the appropriate local body, and this had been speedily granted. The students walked around the graveyard and collected information on age of individuals at death from each gravestone. From the information, they would compile tables showing differential life expectation at birth, divided according to gender and period of history, which would permit longitudinal and lateral comparisons.

What would be revealed? Put bluntly, environment affects life chance, and thus its dark side, death chance too. Life expectation is a revealing composite of and marker for this. Just how long a person lives will vary according to gender, class, area, occupation, genetics and luck. So, in one single afternoon of field-work students were introduced to the notion of life expectation, collected data, compiled a statistical life table, interpreted the results, and related their findings back to environmental and social factors. And the response from my students was very favourable: they said they had learned a lot, learned it well, and enjoyed learning it too. Perhaps I was a teacher, after all!

Later, during employment in Nottingham, and then in London, I plied my trade in the cemeteries of the metropolis amongst Polish war heroes, Chinese take-away proprietors, and a myriad of ordinary dead folk; and learned to deal in what became for me 'living demography'; population geography on the hoof. Indeed, to say it brought the subject to life would be only a modest exaggeration.

And then I made a migration to West Sussex, to the *Costa geriatrica*, to where people come for the sea and the Downs and where, so cynics tell us, they come to await their deaths. And in Bognor Regis I found a population twice as elderly as the national average, and in pockets up to four times as aged.

Bognor Regis, those same cynics cry out: the Tombstone of the Wild South. And it occurred to me that all my life I had been moving south, and now I had run out of land.

So I set out my wares for new students, and introduced my topics in the classroom. And, because this is a subject as arid as a well-powdered oxter, I sold them my case with conviction, with enthusiasm, with - dare I say it ? - panache, for, one misty Friday morning in March, we discovered the Hawthorn Road cemetery; and a colony - nay, a base camp - of forty pioneering students was established on a delicate precipice on the south col shortly after dawn.

VIEW OF HAWTHORN ROAD CEMETERY
Bognor Regis

In reality, it was just after coffee (but let me indulge myself just a touch) and it was at the main entrance. Armed only with clip-boards, Kendal mint-cake and crampons they made their way intrepidly into the heart of darkness. Amid strict instructions not to hunt in large wolf packs, not to disturb those who were visiting graves, and to work quietly and efficiently, they went about their business. And they were as good as gold, for within ninety minutes they had collected data from every possible stone in the cemetery.

And the response, from students who claimed to be agnostic about such a venue, was now much changed: they lamented the sad premature deaths of motor-bike victims; they noted the tragic deaths of mothers and their infants; and they marvelled at the centenarians and wondered if their presence would bias the sample, doubtless exaggerated by selective migration; and demonstrated the notion of an aged local population by showing me just how many elderly were in their sample (overwhelmingly most of them), and responded with polite laughter when I pointed out that, on average, death comes towards the end of the natural life span - and that ideas of a normal distribution curve (for age of death) was, fortunately, improbable.

But then they got the hang of things and began to point out the futility of war, using the numerous graves of young boys as their ammunition, and the extravagance of the late Victorian *nouveau riche* in their determination to secure at least a marble claim on immortality. And they were moved also by the man putting flowers on his wife's grave, and his incessant

TWO TOMBSTONES
HAWTHORN ROAD CEMETERY

moaning about the council's reluctance to cut the grass, for he had nothing else left to say, and no-one to say it to; and impressed by the smart Jewish ghetto in the corner, with its exotic stones somehow redolent of a long dead *Mitteleuropa*; and surprised by the Vietnamese woman's grave next door who had perhaps survived being cast adrift in the South China Sea and almost managed to live out a full ten decades, largely without active intervention from Aneurin Bevan's National Health Service - and thus to end her days far from the killing fields of Indo-China. All this and much more.

Slowly the graveyard gave up its secrets. It revealed an incredible longevity in this corner of Sussex, doubtless accentuated by importation of countless healthy retirees to skew the sample and bias the results. The demographic characteristics locally proved atypical of any national pattern, both now and for the last century. And that women outlived men by a decade or so (for of course they are made tougher than us chaps to withstand the rigours of childbirth and the torment of countless repeats of *The Two Ronnies*); and that in the last half century life expectation has advanced by two decades at birth, so reducing the common spectre (formerly) of the child's grave to a thankfully rare event; and that posh folk get a much better deal than the toiling classes, and that part of the payout for this is extra time accruing to the standard three score years and ten - and much more too, were all revealed.

And how do we know all these things? For when we returned to the classroom, they did their calculations, and compiled their results. And they wrote up their assessments and I read them. I could see that they had without exception understood the demographic processes behind life (and death), but much more too. For here in a small corner of a largely undistinguished town in south-west Sussex was a repository containing the very essence of Life itself, here was the rich tapestry of evidence needed for anyone to teach anything to anyone. Here was the microcosm; here the primary data source. This was Bognor, but could equally well be Baghdad, Benin or Bolivia, for the truths were universal, the encapsulation total, and there for all with eyes to see and a will to understand. Cocooned in the clothes of a single life, yet armed with such a tool, all I had to do was point the way to nurture the inevitable response. Here was the general, there the specific, but together those truths stood out loud and clear. I was home, and Bognor Regis was as splendid a place as any in the world to teach the truths of dying and living.

the bottom and sides: a hollow resonance - the loaf was done! I put it on a rack to cool and stood back. The domed head was smooth, and in the evening light resplendent, golden, and the sides of the loaf were straight and ever so slightly marked, as if they had been wrapped in muslin. But the most amazing image there was the transformation: instead of a pale elastic lump of dough was a shapely form of grand proportions. I weighed it: not quite two pounds, nearer thirty ozs - but close enough for me to say that I had baked a 2 lb. loaf.

The next day (and this was the third, I noticed), I cut some cheese, and went out to find an apple. I chose a Charles Ross: it gave a satisfying hollow sound when tapped, which echoed that of the bread, and weighed, I found, exactly a third of the loaf - 10 ozs.

And then the moment of truth. Taking a knife, I sliced the crust off the loaf: it was moist, and even in texture - the kneading had done its job. I raised it to my mouth. How satisfyingly it ate! Not as good, perhaps, as a loaf baked by Virginia Woolf, who made - so history records - 'beautiful bread';[*] but as I broke into this first slice, the promise of the yeasty, nutty aromas that had filled my mouth for the past days was confirmed - but with this addition, a reassuring 'bite'. Here was a loaf for anyone who aches for the salty substance of 'body', before the flummery and spumy *sfumato* of bread that is sliced, wrapped, anaesthetised.

[*] As reported by Louie Mayer who was cook at Rodmell from 1934 right through to the death of Leonard Woolf in 1969 - see Joan Russell Noble (ed.), *Recollections of Virginia Woolf* (1972).

II

The shingle was in flower, dotted with valerian, thrift and sea-campion, and here and there an early show of the horned poppy and drifts of sea-kale. And twenty miles further east, in what is thought to be a unique site, there would be that rarest of plants, starry clover, already glistening in the morning light. But it was not the eruptions of the shingle that I sought but what lay beyond, so I turned south-west, towards the Bill and, despite a chill wind, quickly fell into conversation.

'Are you here often?' I asked a young girl pushing a buggy.

'Oh, yes, I live here.'

'And this is your child?'

'Yes, this is Luke.'

'That's a fine biblical name,' I replied.

'My husband's choice; he's a fisherman,' came the quick response.

So Fortune smiled, and I seized the opportunity: 'Are you walking far?'

'Oh yes, past the boats and up to the Oval.'

I looked ahead and could see a dozen or so fishing boats drawn up on the shingle and outlined against the ironwork of the Lifeboat Station. 'May I come with you?' I asked. 'I'm just preparing a piece of travel writing about Sussex, and to talk with a fisherman's wife from Selsey would be very helpful.'

'Fine,' she said.

And we set off along the promenade.

Fishing, I learned, is an all year task, and often for seven days a week. The usual pattern was for husband to leave home at four in the morning and not return until noon, after a seven to eight hour trip. In the summer, he worked his own boat, an Orkney fast-liner, built locally and registered at Littlehampton as LI 33; named the *Helen Rebecca,* she had a length of 19ft 6 and weighs just over a tonne.

'Is your name Helen Rebecca, then?' I asked.

'Oh no! Graham bought the boat second-hand and it's bad luck to change a name. Fishing is pretty dangerous - just think of the weight of those pots; catch a line round your ankle when you're laying them over the side - and . . . Doesn't bear thinking about.'

The main fishing at Selsey is for shellfish and piled on the shingle were several heaps of pots. There were two shapes and I discovered that the rounded ones were called 'inkwells', the rectangular - which are much more durable - 'parlours'.

> 'Will you walk into my parlour?' said the fisherman to the lobster;
> there's the saltiest little scad that you ever did espy'[*] - for parlours and other pots must earn their keep.

They cost over thirty pounds apiece, and have a life of only six years - so, along with the boat, there is always on-going expense in maintaining, restoring, and renewing one's equipment.

The fishing grounds are along the coast, mostly to the west and carry, beneath the anonymous water, distinctive names like The Clibs, Nine Fathom, The Strets, Flat Rock, The Hounds - but our path was now off the promenade, up a stony track, and on to what I was told was The Oval, a rectangular patch of ground the size of a small football pitch. Situated immediately behind the Bill, a nondescript promontory of concrete, with a few small groynes stretching out to sea (but, for the curious, provided with steps over each of them), and protected by a few houses, The Oval was a sheltered plateau. On the one side, the ground stretched down a shingle bank to the sea and here and there, amongst the plates of prostrate goosefoot, were dotted clumps of mallow, *Malva sylvestris*, the ivy-shaped leaves glowing against the perfection of the purple veins on the pink petals. 'It's pretty,' she said.

And we set off, back to East Beach.

The most sought-after catch, I was told, are lobster, which come in at just over 1lb in weight, and sell for about £3.50 (summer), £7.00 (winter); but prawns and crab are also valued (did you know that at one time the QEII would only serve *Selsey* crab?), as are bass and, through autumn and early

---

[*]With apologies to Mary Howitt (1799-1888), whose original rhyme related to the proverbial spider and fly. The Bait for lobsters, scad (horse mackerel), is commonly caught locally but also imported from Ireland.

winter, cod.[†]

'It's such a risky business . . . .'

I looked up from my notes and saw we were again near the Lifeboat Station. 'How often are they called out?' I asked.

'No; I mean fishing,' she said. 'And there's no insurance for me and Luke - for seven years if anything happened and Graham wasn't found. Doesn't bear thinking. . . .'

I agreed, and asked about the sheds that were behind the promenade.

'That's the ponds,' she said, 'where they store the crabs and lobsters - they can't be sold on dead, you know.' Although the fleet is not large, about twenty boats in all, the catch is far in excess of local demand and most of it is bought by merchants for selling on to suppliers in France, Spain, and Belgium - all of whom demand their lobster and crab to be . . what should one say, would 'walking dead' be appropriate?

'Does that delay payment?' I asked.

'Oh yes; Graham doesn't get paid for two weeks after landing a catch - which is OK when times are good, but in the winter, if the weather is bad for several weeks . . . ' - and her voice trailed away as she turned landwards.

'You've finished your walk, then?' I said.

'Yes, but Luke likes to see the ducks on the way home - so there's a bit to go yet' - and she bent down, straightened his coat, gave him a kiss and set off down the path, across the corner of a grassy patch, and disappeared through some trees.

'To business', I murmured - and headed towards the huts that were called 'ponds'. Outside sat an elderly figure, 87 year

---

[†] In addition, there are always accidentals; for example, I was told that about twelve years ago Graham found a ling, the largest of the cod family, in one of his inkwells. More recently one of his nets showed a turbot - hooked by a gill. Alas, although he managed to seize it round the thick part of the tail, he was not able to fasten his hands together and it swam away. Distribution maps show that the areas in which such fish are now caught are much reduced, as is the average weight: whereas last century the average weight of a turbot was c. 30 lb, it has now dropped to c. 15 lb; similarly with maximum weights, an outstanding ling last century weighing up to c. 120 lbs, with the maximum to be expected now at only c. 60 lbs.

old Bill Arnell so I later discovered, the doyen of Selsey fishermen - although other fishing families, the Lawrences, Woodlands, Langfords, and Birketts may have other ideas.

'May I look in the ponds?' I asked.

'Go ahead!' and he gestured over his shoulder.

I slipped between his shop and another hut used as a kitchen, and entered a shed with a concrete floor, on which stood a dozen or so tanks. A man, vigorously hosing everything down, brandished a python of a pipe, and I beat a hasty retreat - after glimpsing 50 or so spider crabs in one of the tanks. The shop counter was less threatening . . . and amongst the various fish I saw a heap of prawns. They had been caught that very morning, along the coast beyond Pagham, and had already been cooked. I glanced at my watch - it was only 10.45; Rick Stein would approve - from sea to plate within a few hours; and with prawns in my bag I headed back for the beach.

Finding a sheltered spot, I sat peeling and eating, peeling and eating. There is something gothick about shellfish - all that externality of shell and claw and feeler; but a Selsey prawn, caught, cooked and peeled before the sun has run half its course, is as sweet and welcoming as a Sussex Sue, taut, loquacious, smooth.

III

It was the warmth that beckoned, June's warmth; and although I was not to know this until later, so did the lift and vitality of her embrace.

I had woken early, at about half-six and the deep shadows from the tree outside were already playing on the curtain; reaching out I had flicked it back - and on the instant I was bathed in light and my face began to burn - the sun was so intense. Time for pleasure, I thought, too much is being wasted lying here and dreaming the day away. *And you would agree, too, wouldn't you? It is a day for travel, for a journey.* So I swung out of bed, washed, dressed, and set off over the gravel and up the road.

'Our' road is a mixed community of houses and bungalows, occupied in the main by the retired and semi-retired; but whatever the bias in age, attitudes - if the front gardens are witness - are as varied as in any community: here a dovecote, with a moulded fantail to match the year-round moulded convolvulus in the borders - *at least it's one plant that fails to grow whatever the season. You would like that in your garden. It would be easy-care, don't you think?* - there a tree-mallow, ten feet tall, and further along a purple barberry with a spread of six or more feet to match its height. And then there's the cedar, and the mop-head beech - both reminiscent of another century; a border of cannas, reds and yellows and oranges, some variegated in leaf, others fleshly green but whatever the colour offering spikes of Mexico and Peru to sunny Sussex - for they are plants that originate from central and southern America; and the beech hedge that, low amongst its roots, sparkles in spring with a dance of chinodoxa. *Variety of that order must mean something, surely?* Anyway, round two corners, along the edge of the old tannery with its fifty yards of *Olearia*, New Zealand daisy bush, and up Mount Lane with its double cube, Georgian (founded in 1832) Chapel of St Bartholomew - faced in stone, with the mortar on the south and north elevations studded with gallets, and used now by the Anglican Community of Servants of the Cross, and out to Westgate Fields, that premier of Chichester's several open spaces. *That, at least, is not in dispute, is it?*

Standing on the bridge over a branch of the Lavant, at the head of Mount Lane, I had looked across the grass and set off south-east, for that was where I was heading, towards the station. Ahead was a belt of youthful trees, thick with summer foliage and beyond the Avenue de Chartres multi-storey, the Tuscan red of its brickwork glowing in the

GALLETING ON THE SOUTH WALL OF
ST BARTHOLOMEW'S CHICHESTER

morning light: follow the line of bastions that shield the circular staircases, cross with your eye north, over the walkway to the Roman bastions in the City wall and see how the modern and the ancient sit comfortably together, with the boys and girls from the cathedral school athletically learning, in the shelter between, the skills and assurances of the cricket played by their elders at Arundel or Hove or Ebernoe. And so on to the cycle-track, under the bridge and along the bank of another branch of the Lavant to the station yard and into the concourse that draws one's attention high - to the chandeliers and to the high wall, on sea-blue ground, strewn with plants of field and meadow-vetch, and cranesbill, and ransoms. *Or is that too precise? Perhaps they are only suggestions.* A day-return to Hastings, please, I ask. Yes, I still think of 'Sussex' as the historic Sussex from the Ems to the Wealden Rother, conterminous with the See of Chichester. The journey east, admittedly not quite to the boundary of the county - *Yes, all right, I know Winchelsea and Rye are also in Sussex, but journeying from Chichester to Hastings will give a sense of the whole, and anyway I am not willing to take the train west to Emsworth and then immediately cross the line in order just to come back again, merely for the sake of being a purist; you ask too much - travel writing isn't like that* - will take about two-and-a-half hours, with only a change at Lewes. *What better way to spend a day? Do tell me!*

Travelling by train, as with any other mode, is an experience all its own, with its own opportunities. Freed from the responsibilities of driving (as Kipling found), or pedalling (especially if your route is up the Downs), or piloting (whether boat or plane - as so many did from Sussex harbours and fields more than fifty years ago), or simply just walking (where a church may squat or cuckoo alight), one can just lean back and relax in the train's tubular womb - *Is that your choice, too?* - or take the opportunity to savour the passing world . . . Barnham, Angmering, Goring-by-Sea, Durrington-on-Sea (but with not a wave in sight); West Worthing, Worthing, East Worthing, Lancing, Shoreham-by-Sea, Fishersgate, Aldrington, Hove, Brighton, London Road, Moulescomb, Falmer (with its apt - *so some would think, don't you suspect?* - sign on the platform which asks passengers for the University of Sussex to turn LEFT and those for the University of Brighton to turn RIGHT), and on to Lewes where it was necessary to catch a connection for Hastings. The station itself is being rebuilt, and all the notices - or so it seemed - were obscured by scaffolding, planking and the other needs of modern engineering. But it is lighter than Brighton (where even if one is passing through - *yes, good, I know it is a terminus, with buffers, but some trains do use it as a 'through stop' and travel on to another destination . . . just change seats and you will still be facing forward, although the mirror that I saw you peeping in will now be behind you. Oh! and if you would like fore-warning, the same will happen at Eastbourne* - the dark and gloom is oppressive), and the coffee was warm enough and the connection on time.

And then things changed: there were still names to conjure with - Glynde, Berwick (with its Duncan Grant interior), Polegate, Hampden Park - *the one in Scotland is to do with football* - Eastbourne (light, airy, welcoming: 'Thumping good reads - don't come more gripping than this', the poster shouted - so even if the weather was inclement, the holidaymaker was well provided for. And as for the pier - *oh, yes, every resort that thought it was a resort used to have a pier -* '. . . the hottest talent to cross the Atlantic in years' was in town - *perhaps Eastbourne is not as staid as it would have us think* - Hampden Park (again), Pevensey and West Ham (*what! two of those too?*), Normans Bay, Cooden Beach, Collington - *I don't expect that you ever went to Colindale, did you, where the British Library newspaper archive is held? That's a journey if there ever was one!* - Bexhill, St Leonard's Warrior Square, and so to Hastings.

Listing stations like that makes the journey seem right for an album decorated with intricate patterns of lines and gauges, signals and gradients that gives the entire network of Britain, with space to tick off every stop. But the reality was quite different, for travelling Sussex by train provides what driving the A27 or sailing the shore - *oh! you mean 'Holding the Sextant and the Pen: Sailing the South Saxon Shore' in* Sussex Seams *(1966), a brilliant piece of writing* - seems to miss, an instant appreciation of the pastoral and agricultural present of the county. What, by this mode of travel, is dominant is not the rows of houses and small industrial estates, but the water meadows; the wooded slopes that shield places like Sculpture at Goodwood; the line of the uplands where the South Downs Way runs; the plover, heron, swans and gulls; cattle, horses, rabbits and donkeys; fields of flax, peas, and sweet corn, as well as wheat and barley; and from Falmer to Lewes those rolling downs with a 'shapely figured aspect' which prompted Gilbert White - on one of his many journeys from Selborne via Harting to Ringmer - to exclaim that he always found them 'analogous to growth in their gentle swellings and smooth fungus-like protuberances, their fluted sides, and regular hollows and slopes'. It is a description that applies all along the downs, but especially beyond Lewes from the train, for the scenery quite suddenly becomes less expansive, more homely; less commercialized, more a patchwork of fields and hedges and older crops - hay and field beans, with flocks of sheep, ponds, banks of rushes, marguerites. And again, magically - because it recreates for a brief moment the elation and joy one felt as a child at holiday time - the scenery changes at Normans Bay: in a rattle of wheels as we run along the beach, first by standing - *do you remember peering over Dad's shoulder every August as the loaded car raced to the coast, so as to be the first to cry, 'The sea! the Sea! '* - but then from my seat I could watch the sea-horses galloping to the sands, fishing smacks drawn up on the shingle, and the gulls wheeling and diving 'to the swelling of the voiceful sea'.

But now there was a very different scene. The train had arrived on time at the station - and then across the concourse, over the yard, down the street and through an underpass to the front. Rows of parked cars, notices for tickets and amusements blocked the view, but with the church of St Mary-in-the-Castle (a fine Greek revival, and seemingly built into the rock) on my left I could see in the distance what I had come for - the Net-shops and Hastings Fishermen's Museum. It was only a short step along the promenade, for the wind that had raised the horses at Normans Bay did the rest, and it was a relief to step over the threshold - into a world of ropes and tar; old photos, kit of all sorts; anchors, nets, and fishing records, including a plaice of 20lbs 10ozs, caught locally by Dave Peters in June 1994 in RX 58, *Our Pam and Peter*. And another exhibit caught my eye - a cricket ball netted five miles off Hastings beach only two years ago, affirming a belief that the historians of cricket, whether those of Arundel or Ebernoe, of Eastbourne or Chichester, know only half the story, and that it is the mermen and mermaids of the English deeps who play the better game. But the undulating lift of the plaice began to grow in my mind, and after studying the postcards (mostly of Victorian and Edwardian fishing practice at Hastings) and other literature on the well-stocked table, and buying a substantial history,[*] I stepped out on to the Stade in search of lunch.

It is the Stade, the shingle beach, sheltered from the north by the East Cliff, that forms the focus of the fishing activity. Here, fishermen as long ago as the year of the Spanish Armada (1588) rented space at a farthing a foot to attend to their necessary activities - hauling up the boats from the severity of the weather (first by capstans turned by horses, but now by diesel from small winch-houses); storing and repairing nets, trawls and tackle. It is this last that led to the Net-shops - the rows of tall, three-storied, tarred, wooden

A VIEW OF
HASTINGS HARBOUR
Alan Spencer Brooks

*Steve Park, *Fishermen of Hastings - 200 Years of the Hastings Fishing Community* (Newsbooks, St Leonard's-on-Sea, 1985)

Gaynor Williams

NET-SHOPS
AT HASTINGS

structures that are grouped at the head of the beach. Originally 'shops' where *work* was done, today some are used as an outlet to sell part of the daily catch; but whatever history they have to tell, their strict limitation to a floor space of only eight feet square, speaks of the stricture and constraint of the tasks of a fishermen - at sea as well as on land . . . as it did for others too where land is at a premium, for I was now cosy in the steamy and soft nook of the *Mermaid*. The wind across the Stade had rushed me along quicker than I might have wished, and I was now comfortable at one of only six or so tables in a

c.1586　William CAMDEN, *Britannia,* annotated and edited by Gordon J.
　　　　Copley (Hutchison, 1977)
　　　　Originally published in 1610 the Surrey & Sussex section of this
　　　　perhaps the earliest local topographical description took up 28
　　　　pages (pp.293-321); this edition is based on the 1799 edition
　　　　edited by Richard Gough.

1635　　Lieutenant HAMMOND, *A Relation of a Short Survey of the
　　　　Western Counties Made by a Lieutenant of the Military Company in
　　　　Norwich.* Camden Miscellany, volume VL (Camden Society,
　　　　1936)

1678　　L. CURTIS, *England's Remarques, giving a exact account of the
　　　　several shires, counties and islands in England and Wales* (Langley
　　　　Curtis, 1678)
　　　　General description of the Sussex countryside & industries on
　　　　pp. 189-193; no illustrations.

1694-7　Celia FIENNES, *The Illustrated Journeys of Celia Fiennes,* edited
　　　　and with an introduction by Christopher Morris (MacDonald,
　　　　Webb & Bower, 1982)
　　　　Celia Fiennes (1662-1741) is one of the very few women writers
　　　　of the 17th century & perhaps the earliest travel writer to have
　　　　been published; Sussex is covered briefly, Chichester being
　　　　described in Part I, pp. 62-3, & Rye & Winchelsea in Part II, pp.
　　　　129-30; this volume based on the 1947 Cresset Press edition has
　　　　near contemporary illustrations.

1714　　John MACKY, *A Journey through England, in familiar letters from a
　　　　gentleman here, to his friend abroad* (T. Caldecott, 1714)
　　　　Four further editions were published, the 5th in 1732 comprising
　　　　two volumes.

c.1720-30Thomas COX, *Magna Britannia et Hibernia et Nova, or a New
　　　　Survey of Great Britain.* Volume 5 *Sussex* (publisher unknown,
　　　　n.d.) pp.463-580 covers Sussex.

1724-6　Daniel DEFOE, *A Tour Through the Whole Island of Great Britain*
　　　　[c.1700-1725], edited and with an introduction by Pat Rogers
　　　　(Promotional Reprint Company, 1992; originally published
　　　　1724-1726)
　　　　One of the best known books on the British landscape by one of
　　　　our greatest writers; written in the form of long letters to an

imagined reader; Letter 2, composed probably in 1722, refers at least briefly to most of the large towns in Sussex plus Arundel & Petworth; the appendix to volume 2 describes the parlous state of Sussex roads.

c.1731 John OWEN, *The Traveller's Guide* (publisher unknown, n.d.)
This book is described in *Old Sussex and her Diarists* by A.J. REES (1929); apparently notable for comments on the poor state of Sussex roads.

1750 Richard POCOCKE, *The Travels through England of Dr. Richard Pococke, successively Bishop of Meath and Ossory, during 1750, 1751, and later years* (Camden Society, 1889)

1751 John BURTON, *Journey into Surrey and Sussex. Iter Surriense et Sussexiense Praemittitur de Lingue Graecae Institutionbus Quidbusdam Epistola Critica* (J. & J. Rivington, 1751)
Oxford scholar & clergyman Burton describes in Greek & Latin a journey made in 1751 & remarks particularly on the poor state of the roads & unrefined natives; no illustrations.

1774 William GILPIN, *Observations on the Coasts of Hampshire, Sussex and Kent, relative to picturesque beauty, made in the summer of the year 1774* (Cadell & Davies, 1804)
Gilpin was Prebendary of Salisbury & Vicar of Boldre near Lymington; sections IV to VIII, pp. 27-66, describe a Sussex journey from Chichester Harbour to Rye via Chichester, Goodwood, Halnaker, Arundel, Bury, Petworth, Bramber, Shoreham, Brighton, Lewes, Herstmonceux, Battle & Winchelsea; a few engravings.

1778-9 [Peregrine PHILLIPS] *A Sentimental Diary, Kept in an Excursion to Littlehampton, near Arundel, and to Brighthelmstone, in Sussex in 1778, and also to the latter place in 1779* 2 vols (Ryall & Lee, 1780)
A humorous account with many local details including descriptions of coach travel & sea-bathing.

1782 Antony HIGHMORE, *A Ramble on the Coast of Sussex, 1782* (Reeves & Turner, 1873)
Highmore was a solicitor & author of books on legal, political & social matters; this manuscript was edited by Charles Hindley & describes the coach journey via Horsham & Steyning to Brighton, the ramble around the resort, & the journey to Shoreham, Arundel & Horsham.

1787   Horace WALPOLE, *New and Complete British Traveller* (Alex
        Hogg, 1787)
        Sussex is covered in Chapter II, pp. 39-52, in an 'historical,
        descriptive & biographical survey' by one of the 18th century's
        great writers.

1801   J. EDWARDS, *A Companion from London to Brighthelmston, in*
        Sussex (T. Bensley & J. Edwards, 1801)
        Early descriptions of local places & resorts, notable for numerous
        engravings & especially the superbly drawn & detailed maps,
        showing the coaching road via Horsham, Steyning & Shoreham
        & town plans of Lewes, Shoreham & Steyning.

1801   Thomas PENNANT, *A Journey from London to the Isle of Wight*
        2 vols. (Oriental Press, Wilson & Co., 1801)
        Particularly important for its early descriptions of the resorts,
        some 97 pages in volume 2 cover Sussex from Rye along the
        coast; excellent quality engravings.

1804   Peregrine PROJECT & Timothy TYPE, *A Tour Through Some of the*
        Southern Counties of England (Vernon & Hood, 1804)
        Chapters XI to XIX, pp.146-233, covers West Sussex including
        Emsworth, Chichester, Goodwood, Bognor, Felpham, Arundel,
        Worthing, Steyning & Bramber.

c.1810 G. A. COOKE, *A Topographical and Statistical Description of the*
        County of Sussex (Sherwood, Neely & Jones, n.d.)
        Early descriptions of the emerging resorts; also describes roads
        & rivers, agriculture, industries, markets & fairs etc; crude map
        but no engravings.

1813   *A Guide to all the Watering and Sea-Bathing Places, for 1813*
        (Longman, Hurst, Rees, Orme & Brown, 1813)
        The author is described as 'the editor of the Picture of London';
        includes all the principal seaside resorts plus Chichester &
        Lewes; engravings of Brighton & Rottingdean plus maps of the
        coast & large resorts.

1813   Frederic SHOBERL, *The Beauties of England and Wales, or original*
        delineations, topographical, historical, and descriptive of each County,
        Volume XIV *Sussex* (John Harris, etc., 1813)
        John BRITTON & Edward Wedlake BRAYLEY wrote most of the
        books in this 18 volume series; superb & particularly early

engravings by a variety of artists; another edition with extra
engravings was published in c.1818 by Sherwood, Neely & Jones.

1818   C. WRIGHT, *Rambles in the Vicinity of Brighton* (Sherwood, Neely
       & Jones, n.d.)
Basic guidebook notable for early descriptions of resorts & towns
such as Arundel, Bramber, Eastbourne, Lewes, Shoreham &
Worthing.

1822   [T.K. CROMWELL] *Excursions in the County of Sussex, comprising
brief historical and topographical delineations* (Longman, Hurst,
Rees, Orme & Brown, 1822)
Covers practically all parts of Sussex; 50 descriptions & 50
accomplished engravings by J. Grieg & T. Higham, & others;
maps.

1825   James ROUSE, *The Beauties and Antiquities of the County of Sussex*
2 vols. (J.F. Setchel, 1825)
Consists of 149 sketches by the author who also provided
rudimentary text; a second edition was issued in 1827.

1830   William COBBETT, *William Cobbet's Illustrated Rural Rides 1821-
1832, with economic and political observations*
(Webb & Bower, 1992)
Scattered references to most towns & resorts in Sussex pp.72-88;
first published in 1830, later editions include 1853, 1885 & 1908.

c.1830   [George MOGRIDGE] *Old Humphrey's Country Strolls* (Religious
Tract Society, n.d.)
Notable mainly for its early descriptions of the relatively new
resorts of Brighton & Worthing.

1833   J.D. PARRY, *An Historical and Descriptive Account of the Coast of
Sussex* (Wright & Sons, 1833)
Includes 17th & 18th century surveys & accounts of journeys;
covers towns & villages up to 10 miles inland eg. Lewes &
Steyning.

1835   H. DUDLEY, *Juvenile Researches, or a description of some of the
principal towns in the West of Sussex, and the borders of Hants.* (H.
Dudley, 2nd ed. 1835)
Basic contemporary & historical descriptions; some crude
drawings, by the author.

c.1835 H. Gastineau N. WHITTOCK, *The Picturesque Beauties of the Counties of Surrey & Sussex* (George Virtue, n.d.)
A series of original drawings by Whittock, engraved with great skill by others plus a page of text; covers most of the principal Sussex towns, the usual selection of churches, castles & general views.

c.1840 G.N. GODWIN, *The Green Lanes of Hampshire, Surrey and Sussex* (Griffiths & Farron, n.d.)
Focuses on the Sussex/Hampshire/Surrey border area around Lynchmere, Shulbrede, Hollycombe & Milland; one chapter on King Charles II's route through Sussex in 1651.

1849 [J.B. DASHWOOD] *A Handbook of Travel Round the Southern Coast of England* (Nattali, 1849)
Written unashamedly to attract the new "railroad tourists", the text takes the format of 'Letters' each covering several days of travel along a part of the South Coast; Letter III describes Rye to Rottingdean; Letter IV Brighton to Bognor; Letter V Chichester to Southampton; 124 pp out of 324 are local; 35 engravings by Collins, Dewint, Owen, Prout & Turner; also re-printed shortly afterwards under the title *The Southern Coast of England*.

1859 Mackenzie WALCOTT, *A Guide to the Coast of Sussex* (Edward Stanford, 1859)
A basic guidebook, the text from which, judging by the pagination (pp. 125-262), was originally part of a larger work.

1867 J.B. DASHWOOD, *The Thames to the Solent by Canal and Sea, or the log of the Una boat 'Caprice'* (Longmans & Green, 1868)
Fascinating account of what must have been one of the last horse-drawn boat journeys from Weybridge to the Solent via the Wey & Arun canal during 1867; seven drawings plus two sketch maps; Shepperton Swan published a facsimile reprint in 1980.

1877 Louis J. JENNINGS, *Field Paths and Green Lanes in Surrey and Sussex* (John Murray, 4th ed. 1877, re-printed 1884)
Covers areas around Hastings, Rye & Winchelsea, Crowhurst & Etchingham, Bodiam, Herstmonceux & Pevensey, Mayfield, Alfriston & Wilmington, Pulborough to Bramber via Storrington, Haywards Heath to East Grinstead, Petworth to Midhurst to Haslemere; seven sketches by J.W. Whymper.

1880   Louis J. JENNINGS, *Rambles Among the Hills, in the Peaks of*
         Derbyshire and the South Downs (Murray, 1880)
         Designed to complement his volume *Field Paths* (previous page);
         Part II (pp 149-289) covers Sussex.

1884   John Coker EGERTON, *Sussex Folk and Sussex Ways*
         (Methuen, 1884)
         Descriptions & anecdotes of rural folk, gleaned during Egerton's
         travels, particularly in the Burwash area; 2nd & 3rd editions were
         published in 1892 & 1924 respectively.

1887   James John HISSEY, *A Holiday on the Road, an artist's wanderings*
         in Kent, Sussex and Surrey (Richard Bentley, 1887)
         A literary & pictorial account of a journey by horse & phaeton
         (four-wheeled open carriage); covers areas around Alfriston,
         Battle, Beachy Head, Birling, Bodiam, East Dean, Eastbourne,
         Friston, Herstmonceux, Mayfield, Michelham, Pevensey,
         Robertsbridge, Seaford & Wilmington; 44 engravings &
         woodcuts by the author.

1892   See also 1884 EGERTON and 1906 HARPER

1893   Edward F. SKINNER, *A Handbook of Sussex, for the pocket, the*
         library or the tea table (John Haddon, 1893)
         Basic guidebook, little literary merit; 22 drawings.

c.1895   Clare JERROLD, *Picturesque Sussex* (Valentine, n.d.)
         A basic guidebook, notable mainly for its 40 good quality
         Victorian photographs.

1896   Augustus J.C. HARE, *Sussex* (George Allen, 2nd ed. 1896)
         Standard late Victorian guidebook; unusual & attractive
         illustrations; the first edition was published in 1894.

1896   James John HISSEY, *On Southern English Roads*
         (Richard Bentley, 1896)
         A substantial account of a 467 mile journey by horse & dog-cart
         (two-wheeler); despite the title 15 of the 22 chapters cover most
         areas of Sussex away from the coast; the circular route runs from
         Eastbourne to Crowborough, East Grinstead, Horsham, Steyning,
         Petworth, Midhurst & back through Chichester, Arundel,
         Worthing, Lewes & Seaford; 16 particularly fine drawings by the
         author & a map.

1900   See also 1909 BRABANT

c.1900   Hilaire BELLOC, *The Four Men* (Tom Stacey, 1971)
            This fictional account of a walk around 1900 from Robertsbridge
            to Harting is one of the classic Sussex novels & was first
            published in 1902; it was also the inspiration for one of the finest
            pieces of post-war travel writing *Across Sussex with Belloc, in the
            footsteps of the 'Four Men'* by Bob Copper (Alan Sutton, 1994) who
            walked the same route in 1950 & 1984.

1901   F.G. BRABANT, *Sussex* (Methuen, 1901)
            A conventional guide book arranged alphabetically by place,
            with introductory sections on geography, climate, natural history
            etc; notable chiefly for drawings by Edmund H. New, & a map.

1901   T.C. WOODMAN, *The South Downs* (Hove Gazette, 1901)
            Divided into two parts: firstly a literary sketch, then a
            topographical description of each rape, parish by parish; useful
            list of hills & their heights; not illustrated; a second edition was
            published by H. & C. Treacher in 1902;

1902   Michael FAIRLESS, *The Roadmender* (Duckworth, 1902)
            The first edition of this devotional classic was reprinted 26 times
            in its first nine years & several later editions followed; written in
            the first person we follow the fictional journeys of a roadmender
            in the countryside around Ashurst, Bramber, Cowfold, Edburton,
            Henfield, Shermanbury, Shoreham & Steyning; Michael
            FAIRLESS was the pen name of Margaret Fairless BARBER, born
            in Yorkshire but who lived latterly at Shermanbury, near
            Henfield.

1903   Duncan MOUL, & W.J. HARDY, *Picturesque Sussex*
                (Robinson, 1903)
            Over 70 superb turn-of-the century sketches dominate the rather
            basic text; all parts of Sussex are covered except the coast from
            Bognor to Eastbourne.

1904   E.V. LUCAS, *Highways and Byways in Sussex* (Macmillan, 1904)
            Covers all areas of the County; interesting for comments made in
            the 2nd edition (1935) on the effects of modern technology on the
            Sussex landscape described in the first; 80 drawings by Frederick
            L. Griggs, R.A.

1906 Hilaire BELLOC, *Sussex* (A. & C. Black, 1906)
Colour paintings by Wilfred Ball are a principal feature; although not credited to him, the text is by Belloc & this guide is one of the classics; a second edition was published in 1925 & an updated version was published by Cassell in 1936 under the title *The County of Sussex*.

1906 Martin COBBETT, *Wayfaring Notions* (Sands, 1906)
This well-known sports journalist was born & bred in Brighton; includes an account of the author's life & describes journeys around Angmering, Brighton to Newhaven, the Downs, Eastbourne, Goodwood, Lewes, Patching, Plumpton, road milestones, Rye & Selsey; no illustrations except a portrait of the author.

1906 Charles G. HARPER, *The Brighton Road, speed, sport, and history on the classic highway* (Chapman & Hall, 2nd edition 1906)
One of the classic travel books; although first published in 1892 the second edition is much fuller regarding text, illustrations & sketch maps; 50 separate plates & 31 within the text most by the author; excellent on coaching matters; a 3rd edition appeared in 1922; a miniature version (3.5" x 2.25") edition was also published by Treherne & Co. in 1906.

1906 Charles G. HARPER, *The Hastings Road, and the 'happy springs of Tunbridge'* (Chapman & Hall, 1906)
Another classic, of similar quality to The Brighton Road (see above); 18 separate plates & 49 within the text, most by the author.

1909 Arthur BECKETT, *The Spirit of the Downs, impressions and reminiscences of the Sussex Downs* (Methuen, 1909)
An Edwardian classic by the founder of the *Sussex County Magazine*; includes 20 colour paintings by Stanley Inchbold.

1909 F.G. BRABANT, *Rambles in Sussex* (Methuen, 1909)
A more detailed version of the *Little Guide to Sussex* published in 1900; all towns & their district are covered; includes 24 Frith & Valentine photographs & six J.M.W. Turner paintings, & two maps.

1933   Walter WILKINSON, *A Sussex Peep-Show* (Geoffrey Bles, 1933)
The adventures enjoyed by the puppeteers of a travelling Punch
& Judy show, transported by barrow, are described in a
meandering route from Rudgwick to Birling Gap; no
illustrations.

1935   See also 1904 LUCAS and c.1910 THE TRAMP

1935   A.A. EVANS, *A Saunterer in Sussex* (Methuen, 1935)
Twenty-five chapters cover the Adur valley, Alfriston, Barpham,
Chiddingly, Cuckmere, Didling, Egdean, Glynde, Pagham,
Penhurst, Pevensey, Pynham Priory, Thorney Island, Tortington,
Waldron & Withyham; themes include birds, church art & scratch
(sun) dials, Richard Cobden, gipsies, mystery plays & standing
stones; illustrated by 19 photographs.

1936   See also 1906 BELLOC

1936   George AITCHISON, *Sussex* (A. & C. Black, 1936)
One of the many inter-war guides; remarkable mainly for the
colour illustrations painted by Wilfred Ball, R.E..

1936   Esther MEYNELL, *Sussex Cottage* (Chapman & Hall, 1936)
In Chapters III, IV & V this accomplished local writer describes
various villages north of the Downs, Lewes & district, & the
South Downs themselves; 16 notable black & white photographs.

1937   Arthur MEE, *The Kings England, Sussex, the garden by the sea*
          (Hodder & Stoughton, 1937)
Comprehensive architectural survey of 300 places, illustrated by
238 contemporary photographs.

1938   R. Thurston HOPKINS, *Sussex Rendezvous*
          (Skeffington, n.d. [1938])
A series of rambles around places & themes: included are the
Adur river, Arundel, Brighton, Eastbourne to Lewes, Frant to
Brightling, Goodwood, Hastings, Horsham, Pallingham Quay
(Wey & Arun canal), Parham, archeological sites, castles, ghosts
& windmills.

1938   S.C. KENDALL, *The Sussex County Book*
          (Lindsay Drummond, 1938)
Comprehensive survey of Sussex (386 pages) just before World

War II; includes sections on agriculture, education, iron industry, personalities & sport.

1939   A.A. EVANS, *By Weald and Down* (Methuen, 1939)
This standard guide has 24 chapters organized by place & subject; particularly featured are Amberley, Birling, Cocking, East Dean, Fairlight, Fletching, Ford, Friston, Kirdford, Otham Abbey, Pagham, Pevensey, Rye, Tillington, West Chiltington & Wilmington; subjects include bells, bridges, church graffiti, Downs, gypsies, inns, nature & parish registers

1939   S.P.B. MAIS, *Hills of the South* (Southern Railway Company, n.d.)
Beautifully written & economical prose by one of the great travel writers; arranged in a series of walks, Sussex is covered in pp.7-46; unusual colour paintings by Audrey Weber, maps by Helen Ray Marshall.

1942   H.V. MORTON, *I Saw Two Englands, the record of a journey before the War, and after the outbreak of war, in the year 1939* (Methuen, 1942)
A last glimpse of pre-war Sussex by an accomplished writer; chapters 4 & 5 describe Sussex, & especially Alfriston, Arundel,Battle, Bignor, Chichester, Fittleworth, Lewes, Midhurst & Pyecombe; five local photographs.

1942   Nancy PRICE, *Jack By The Hedge* (Muller, 1942)
This West End actress lived for many years at High Salvington, Worthing; this substantial account of her adventures when she reverted to type & joined "the brotherhood of the road" includes pre-war photographs of the characters & scenes she encountered.

1946   Ruth COBB, *A Sussex Highway* (Epworth Press, 1946)
A charming account of the road from Lewes to Clayton via Offham, Plumpton, Westmeston & Ditchling; 20 drawings by the author.

1947   Esther MEYNELL, *Sussex* (Hale, 1947)
A standard post-war guide with thematic chapters; 49 disappointing black & white photographs & a map.

1947   Reginald TURNER, *Sussex* (Vision of England Series) (Paul Elek, n.d.)
Notable only for the unusual pen & ink drawings by Michael Rothenstein.

1949   S. B. MAIS, *The Land of the Cinque Ports*
        (Christopher Johnson, 1949)
        Part II covers Sussex, i.e. Rye, Winchelsea & Hastings; 14
        distinctive Sussex drawings by Rowland Hilder.

1949   Hardiman SCOTT, *Secret Sussex* (Batchworth Press, 1949)
        Slightly eccentric but nonetheless interesting accounts of people
        & places immediately after the war (1947-8) a period not well
        covered; includes Alfriston, Arundel, Boxgrove, Burgess Hill,
        Buxted, Cowfold, Easebourne, Ebernoe, Emsworth, Hardham,
        Harting, Henfield, Lindfield, Northchapel, Trotton & Westergate.

CONTRIBUTORS

CHRIS AGGS teaches painting and printmaking in the Fine Art Department at University College Chichester. He exhibits regularly in London and lives in West Sussex.

GEORGE APPLEBY teaches in Further Education and is President of the New Park Centre, Chichester.

ROGER BAMBER works for *The Guardian*; based in Brighton, he covers stories on the South Coast. He was British Press Photographer of the Year in 1973, 1983 and 1992.

TONY BARNES, formerly Principal Lecturer in Education at Chichester Institute of Higher Education, has published several hundred photographs in magazines and books, including *Photography Year Book* (Fountain Press, 1990 and 1992).

JACKIE BARTLETT has written since childhood. She loves the countryside and natural world, and used to enjoy living in Chichester before her present post as warden of a Quaker Meeting House on the Wirral.

DENISE BENNETT lives in Portsmouth. Her first collection of poetry will be published by Flarestack in December 1999.

BRIAN CAWS retired from West Sussex Institute of Higher Education in 1989 - where he held office as Dean of Students and (earlier) Dean of Humanities. He is now Chief Examiner for Advanced Level English Literature for University of London Examinations. He is a keen cricketer at club and village level, and used to captain the Hampshire County Under-19 XI.

TIM CHILCOTT, formerly Dean of Faculty of Arts and Humanities (Chichester Institute of Higher Education), is an authority on the work of John Clare. His *John Clare: the Year 1841* will be published by Trent Editions in autumn 1999.

RILLA DUDLEY is Librarian at Durrington High School.

ANDREW FLAHERTY is Manager at Cairnsmore, Chichester; as well as mountain-riding, he enjoys climbing, sailing and walking.

CHARLES FOSTER lives on the edge of Chichester Harbour; he is preparing a sketchbook of forms on the margins of the harbour.

PATRICK GARLAND is a former Artistic Director at Chichester Festival Theatre; his *The Incomparable Rex: a Memoir of Rex Harrison in the 1980s* was published last year and is now in paperback.

JANE GERMAN, a former teacher in West Sussex, now lives in the Waveney Valley, Norfolk; she exhibits regularly in London, East Anglia, and West Sussex. Her work is featured in *Country Living* (September 1999).

JOHN GODFREY is Assistant County Secretary for West Sussex County Council.

DAVID GUTTERIDGE teaches at Bishop Luffa, Chichester, and is Secretary of the Chichester Cathedral Choristers' Association.

MARTIN HAYES is Principal Librarian (Local Studies) for West Sussex County Council Library Service. He is based at Worthing.

PHILIP HUGHES, artist, is Chairman of the Board of Trustees, National Gallery, and Director of Thames and Hudson; he exhibits regularly, notably at the Francis Kyle Gallery (London). He was co-founder of Logica.

PETER IDEN, artist, is based in Chichester, where his exhibitions are a keenly-anticipated event in the annual calendar.

SYD KELLY is a former teacher of Geography; he has a particular interest in change in the landscape and has recently written a study of identity in the Isle of Man.

TIMOTHY J. McCANN is Assistant County Archivist at West Sussex County Record Office and Chairman of the Editorial Board of *Sussex Archaeological Collections*.

MOLLY MAHOOD, formerly a professor of English in Nigeria and Tanzania, is Emeritus Professor at University of Kent (Canterbury). Her publications include *Shakespeareís Wordplay* (1957) and *Playing Bit Parts in Shakespeare* (1998). She is an active campaigner for environmental issues and an authority on plant lore, especially in the poetry of John Clare.

JULIAN MARSHALL combines research into Victorian life styles (especially those in Victorian cotton mills, and at Girton) with painting and printmaking; work from her Itchenor studio has recently been exhibited in London, Snape, Amersham, and Lymington.

SIR MICHAEL MARSHALL, D.L., was MP for Arundel (1974-97); he is Chairman of Chichester Festival Theatre Trust and a Trustee of University College Chichester. His *Cricket at the Castle: One Hundred Years of cricket at Arundel 1895-1995* was published in 1995.

ERIC JAMES MELLON, artist, is an innovator in painting on ceramics; he also specializes in using ash glazes.

DIANA MITCHENER has lived in Ifold for over thirty years; prior to her recent retirement, she was on the staff at the Centre for International Education and Management, University College Chichester.

STEPHANIE NORGATE teaches English at University College Chichester, where she leads the MA in Creative Writing. As well as being a poet, Stephanie writes for the radio and her *Clive* was broadcast on Radio 4 last December.

MAGGIE ROBERTS, a trained nurse, psychiatric and general, is planning a world tour in 2000 - Thailand, Tasmania, New Zealand, Fiji and Los Angeles.

JOHN SAUNDERS, a specialist in the work of Shakespeare, teaches literature and Related Arts at University College Chichester where he initiated Creative Writing programmes at both undergraduate and graduate level.

MAGGIE SAWKINS teaches in Further Education and is currently working on a sequence of poems about the Irish Famine of the 1840s.

WENDY SCOTT, former Deputy Director of Chichester Institute of Higher Education (now University College Chichester), lives north of the Downs. She has travelled extensively over recent months - in Japan, in the Middle East, and in South Africa but still finds mystery in the Sussex countryside.

CHRISTOPHER SMITH is Head of Geography at University College Chichester; in a previous post he was on the staff at University of Nottingham Medical School investigating the health care of the elderly.

CHRIS SPARKES has published in several magazines and anthologies, including *Grandchildren of Albion* (1992); he writes also in the field of biblical studies and has just prepared a study of concepts of the soul.

SPENCER THOMAS, a former Head of Geography at Bognor Regis College (later Chichester Institute of Higher Education), is widely known for writing both textbooks and academic articles.

NICK WARBURTON is a prolific writer for radio (BBC and ITV) and also for children; the British Library catalogue records 42 items over the past fifteen years.

CHRIS WATERS is National Trust Officer (Education) for the Cuckmere Valley; he also teaches in Adult Education.

JOY WHITING, who formerly taught at Midhurst Intermediate School, has a keen interest in sites that inspire writers; she was photographer for *An Arundel Tomb* (1989), an analysis of Philip Larkin's poem based on the tomb in Chichester Cathedral.

GAYNOR WILLIAMS teaches Art History in Further Education and has especial expertise in the art of the present century, as well as in that of the Renaissance.

ANNE WILLIAMSON manages the literary estate of Henry Williamson and has published *Henry Williamson: Tarka and the Last Romantic* (1995) and *Henry Williamson and the First World War* (1998).

RICHARD WILLIAMSON, who has worked in nature conservation for more than a generation, has written a column about the natural scene for the *Chichester Observer*, weekly, for thirty-six years.

JOHN WYATT was the first Director (1977-97) of the West Sussex (later, Chichester) Institute of Higher Education. He is a specialist in understanding the intellectual environment of the Romantics, and his *Wordsworth and the Geologists* was published in 1995. In the earlier volume, *Sussex Seams* (1996), he wrote about Charlotte Smith (1749-1806), the Sussex novelist and sonneteer.

ACKNOWLEDGEMENTS

To turn an idea for a journey into a physical and graspable reality is sometimes fraught with risk - missed connections, cancelled flights, unruly companions, may all interrupt what was planned as purposeful and exciting. In this instance, however, the contrary has occurred - the companionship of contributors, realized and potential, has been stimulating (although I am sad that a number stepped off the train en route), and arrival at the various necessary stops has, in most instances, been on time; further, as I now see the terminus of our endeavours, I believe that all who have shared the journey will find the destination to be full of interest and that, as we explore and re-explore its forty (and more) streets, vistas, and other locations everyone will feel the outlay of participation to have been both rewarding and worthwhile.

For funding the venture I wish to record thanks to Dr Christopher Smith, who was first to suggest, as long ago as 16 May 1996, some kind of sequel to *Sussex Seams* - which had been launched that very day; to Dr Andrew Foster, Chair of the Research Committee at University College Chichester; and to my colleagues in this volume who hold office within the West Sussex County Council - notably, Martin Hayes, with whom I first shared the possibility of a joint publication, Timothy J. McCann who willingly gave his support, and Dr John Godfrey who has encouraged the endeavour at every stage.

For the provision of research facilities I am grateful to Philip E. D. Robinson, Director, University College Chichester; and I wish also to record my appreciation of assistance from library and technical staff in the Learning Resource Centre at UCC - on several occasions they were able to ensure that I was on the right platform and knew which connection I needed.

Finally, I thank Dr Brian Short for acting as Consultant to the project; Ian Elliott for preparing such an encouraging Foreword; Shaun Payne for assisting with the epigraphs; and Susannah Foreman, Vivienne Frost, and Di Burford for help with editing and other, often unspoken, tasks. Every contributor will, I think, have personal thanks to make to one or more helpers in the preparation of their own contribution - and I should be glad if they would convey also my own appreciation: what is unseen is often as significant as, if not more so than, what is seen.

Published

2000
(November 1999)

by

University College Chichester
Bishop Otter Campus
Chichester
West Sussex
PO19 4PE

in association with

West Sussex County Council

ISBN 0-948765-14-3

Designed and printed by

Bexley Printers Ltd
PETWORTH